One Life To Ride

A Motorcycle Journey to the High Himalayas

Reprint 2023

FiNGERPRINT!
An imprint of Prakash Books India Pvt. Ltd.

113/A, Darya Ganj, New Delhi-110 002,
Tel: (011) 2324 7062 – 65, Fax: (011) 2324 6975
Email: info@prakashbooks.com/sales@prakashbooks.com

facebook www.facebook.com/fingerprintpublishing
twitter www.twitter.com/FingerprintP, www.fingerprintpublishing.com

ISBN: 978 81 7599 294 8

Processed & printed in India by HT Media Ltd, Greater Noida

One Life To Ride

A Motorcycle Journey to the High Himalayas

AJIT HARISINGHANI

FINGERPRINT!

Praise for *One Life to Ride*

'This is a rare book . . . the rider is on the road to enlightenment. In lean elegant prose, he makes Robert Pirsig's cerebral Zen motorbike classic seem passé. *One Life to Ride* is a humane study by an author in command of both the nuts and bolts of his 350cc partner and a guaranteed formula to get the rest of us out of our self-ordained rut.'

— **Bill Aitken, *Outlook Traveller***

'What makes the book captivating is its tireless endeavour to bring India and its remote areas alive in the minds of readers who may never get a chance to go there and meet the different people who make up the rich diversity of the land. Peppered with humour, the narrative touches emotions, characters, and thoughts to make for a compelling read.'

— ***The Indian Express***

'The book is a breeze . . . for the simplicity of its language, the fun of adventure, the droll humour. One can feel the exhilaration and the exhaustion by turns.'

— ***DNA***

'By the time you finish, you feel you've made a friend. Harisinghani's writing comes from the heart and reading his book, you get a clear sense of an uncomplicated, sincere guy with easy priorities and no hang-ups. Rated 7/10.'

—**Saaz Agarwal, *Mid Day***

'*One Life to Ride* traverses the landscape of courage, life, God. As you ride pillion, a truly curious and vivid experience is yours to savour. Ajit's writing is clear, simple and strong . . . like his Enfield's *dugh . . . dugh*. You really can't put it down.'

— ***Deccan Herald*, Bangalore**

'*One Life to Ride* is a fantastically consolidated journey, one that made me laugh, hold my breath, caution against high-altitude sickness whilst curled up on my sofa and thank all the lords above that there are some journeys you just do not need a visa for.'

— **Reem Wasey, Asst. Editor, *Daily Times*, Pakistan**

'An entrancing travelogue . . . Once the journey begins, the witty, incisive reflections give the reader a feeling of actually being there with the author. Just not to be missed.'

— **Twist 'n Tales Bookstore, Pune**

'Ajit Harisinghani proves his bike can be a purring kitten as well as a rancorous lover. *One Life to Ride* grips you with awe and hilarity and spirituality and atheism equally. That's the balance.'

—**Dr. Geeta Koppikar, Director,**
Breach Candy Hospital, Mumbai

'It was a fast read and very enjoyable. What a great opportunity to have the time and desire to travel so extensively. The only things that I know of India are what I read or see on TV which of course usually show the crowded cities or the Taj Mahal. I really enjoyed the peace and tranquillity as well as some excitement along the way. I know I will never be able to see your great country but you certainly whet my appetite to know more.'

— J. Collins, Pennsylvania, USA

'*One Life to Ride* is a book, definitely under the 'unputdownable' category . . . brilliant nuggets of wisdom disguised as casual remarks or plain homilies. The book can convert any person into a motorcycle enthusiast.'

— Max Babi, poet and physicist, Pune

'*One Life to Ride* is a fast, enjoyable read. If you ever have the desire to abandon your fears and take a journey across country, do it. With a little faith, a sense of humour and a lot of common sense, the trip will be a success. And be sure to read *One Life to Ride* before you embark on your journey!'

— City Masala, Florida, USA

'A book for the armchair traveller as well as the biker, this old-fashioned travelogue is equal parts thought bubbles, checklists, ramblings and mind epiphanies, steering clear of coolio-bravado.'

— *First City*, New Delhi

'India seems a mythical land to the rest of us, and we could never hope to understand such a deep and complex world even if we took 1,000 journeys across the vast sub-continent. But Mr. Harisinghani has spun a wonderful narrative of a journey where you're riding pillion on a 4,300 kilometre adventure from Pune in west-central India all the way north. It's fun, exciting, spiritual with a sense of humour and you'll learn a lot about a fantastic and varied country. Highly recommended.'

— **Rick Burns,** ***webbikeworld.com***

'Very honest and inspiring.'

— **Shamim Akhtar, author of *Rode to Heaven – Ladakh.***

'What adds flavour to this book and makes it different from a normal travelogue is Ajit's ability to not only depict road trip, but also the journey taking place in his mind, as he shares his witty comments, past experiences and thoughts with his readers. And this I feel is an important part of the book, as travelling is not only about exploring the world; it is also about exploring yourself as a person.'

— **Yogesh Sarkar,** ***www.yogeshsarkar.com***

'Ajit's is a journey of passion and energy and his narration of it is so vivid and compelling that I found myself riding pillion. With him I could experience the loneliness of the long-distance rider; with him I was filled with wonder at the yogi's story, and with him I cried after meeting young soldiers and wondered if they would ever return home. This book is truly startling in the range of emotions it evokes.'

— Indira Chowdhury, historian, ***www.archindia.org***

'Now here's a brilliantly talented writer who, with no great prior preparedness, has the guts and gumption to bike across from one end of the country to the other, ready to deal with situations as they emerge and tell us things we rarely hear about this wonderful land called India. *One Life to Ride* is a marvellous book. I haven't read anything better in a long long time.'

— K.D. Krishnanand, literary critic, California

This book is dedicated to

J. R. D. Tata

A karmayogi who was really a romantic at heart.

Contents

Prologue

Even after the stroke left him half paralyzed and robbed him of much of his speech, Jeremy D'Costa was an impressive presence. There was a certain dignity about the manner in which he gripped his four-legged aluminium walking stick as he got out of the back seat of his black Mercedes and struggled to make his way to the front door of the clinic. Tall, dusky and suave, dressed in clothes that had come from the best known brands, he looked what he was, a successful and polished man of the corporate world. Facial palsy had skewed the symmetry of his features but he still managed to look benign and handsome.

His visiting card said he was CEO of Ace Electrodes but since his stroke, his work had been taken over by a Mr. Desai, his assistant, in what was said to be a purely temporary arrangement until the boss recovered.

As his speech therapist, it was obvious to me that the day of his supposed return to his office was a distant dream.

His stroke had left him severely handicapped. Aside from the physical disability it had caused to the right half of his body, it had damaged his memory circuits, which store the basic concepts of human language and speech.

Six months of speech therapy sessions had helped him regain a portion of his communication abilities, but he still had a long way to go. A man who had been an expert at high-level finance was now just about able to add single digit numbers. Where once his intelligent and witty conversation had held the attention of the rich and famous, he now found great difficulty in putting together simple five-word sentences. But improving he surely was, considering he had not been able to say a single word for the first two months of therapy.

Brain strokes frequently cause severe disturbances of intellectual functions. Abstract thinking, analytical abilities that process data, emotional parity… everything that is intimate about personality is altered. Family members find it difficult to come to terms with this new person who has replaced the one they knew. Mr. D'Costa had two sons, both living abroad, so it was his wife, Esther, who had to look after her husband. At 60, Esther D'Costa had taken on serving her husband with the zeal of a martyr. She made sure he took all his pills regularly, accompanied him to hospital for his weekly physical checks, and policed his diet to make sure he did not eat anything other than what the doctors permitted. Roles had reversed. The dominant male had been reduced to meek subservience and needed time to accept the change. Mr. D'Costa, who had prided himself on his independence, hated the fact that his wife was now making decisions for him, that he needed her help for everything from going to the toilet, to getting dressed.

The prolonged unrelenting pressure also began to tell on her and she was close to a nervous breakdown. I could see that Mr. D'Costa blamed himself for the condition his normally cheerful wife had been reduced to. As his conversational abilities began to re-emerge, he often talked of how guilty he felt and how much it worried him. I listened to him vent his frustrations, and tried to swerve him back to feeling good about himself. He was gradually becoming aware of the extent of his disability and this awareness often brought tears to his eyes. Tears of exasperation, anger and helplessness.

Mr. D'Costa began to talk more freely but not with anyone else.

I became the only person in the world he felt comfortable enough with, to attempt putting words together.

His speech was staccato and often he'd lose the

thread of his thoughts mid-sentence. Then a smile of apology would appear.

'Mr. Doc... Today... No... Yesterday...Mr. Sinha... Ashok... Evening,' he'd say and I'd understand his staff had visited him the previous evening. But when I checked (as I often did) with Mrs. D'Costa, it would appear that actually these people were to come the next day.

With the passing of a few more weeks, there were some noteworthy improvements. His verbal expression increased.

As so often happens with stroke cases, recent memories are forgotten but recollecting older events is easier. I began to ask him about his student days which I knew he had spent in Germany. He told me about the German girls he'd met. How he had taken his friend Ingrid on his BMW motorcycle all the way to the south of Italy.

He had been as passionate about his BMW as I am about my Enfield. So the two of us got along like a bushfire, which I saw was helping his therapy too. Six months later, Mr. D'Costa had not fully recovered but was leaving Pune for San Francisco to live with his son's family for a year. A rehab centre, which specialized in treating stroke patients, had agreed to evaluate his case and suggest advanced therapy procedures which had shown promising results in many other similarly afflicted people.

When he came for his last session, Mr. D'Costa brought me a gift. It was a book, *Keynote,* written by JRD Tata. Industrialist, pioneer flyer, racer of fast cars and a charmer of beautiful women, JRD was Mr. Maximum to me. Mr. D'Costa had met JRD several times and was as ardent an admirer of his as I was. Opening the book, he pointed to a line he had highlighted in yellow:

... the thrill and sense of self-fulfilment obtained from living a little dangerously.

'Doc,' he began in his slow and laboured manner, 'I am ... going.'

'You'll have fun with all those American women,' I replied in the off-hand facetious manner, which always brought a smile to his face.

'What are you… when are you…. adventure… do it for me. Motorcycle.'

What he was asking was whether I was actually going on the cross-country motorcycle trip that we had often talked about.

'Yes. Mr. D'Costa, I will do it. For you and for me.'

He extended his good left hand and shook mine.

'Have a safe trip, Mr. D'Costa,' I said and walked him to his car. For the last time, as it turned out.

Three days later, just a day before he was to leave

for the US, Mr. D'Costa died in his sleep. His wife said he looked very peaceful in death.

Machinophilia

My love affair with the Royal Enfield began 30 years ago when a chance ride on a friend's machine convinced me that it was exactly the motorcycle I was looking for. I liked its classic look and the deep dugh… dugh… dugh sound of its engine. 'Everyone makes way for an Enfield' the ads said and I believed them and got myself one.

With its engine design unchanged from a decade after World War II, the Enfield has often been unfavourably compared with the newer motorcycles, which, with their lighter frames, greater fuel efficiency and reliability of performance promise a better deal. But to an Enfield lover, that's like comparing mangoes with potatoes. The Enfield I've realized, is really a temperamental woman disguised as a motorcycle and ours is not a relationship of convenience. Sometimes she can be adamant and uncooperative and very difficult to reason with. She can sense my moods and even my intentions. Once, attracted to a more advanced model, I had considered a trading alliance with her. The modern motorcycle beckoned me enticingly from billboards and newspapers in full seductive colour. I visited the showroom and took a test ride on the sleeker machine. This new one felt different. Lighter and easily excited into full flight with her '0 to 100 in x seconds' flat! To an Enfield, that's premature ejaculation. It was staying power she valued. But I was enamoured with my new liaison and had no ears for her wisdom.

Later, standing next to my Enfield, I remember talking to a friend, clinically weighing the pros and cons of possessing the shiny Japanese model. Right in her presence too! In the week that followed, she behaved exceptionally well. She'd purred smoothly into life at the hint of a kick from my foot. She used up less gas, surged into full flight at the mere flexing of my right wrist. That week she'd performed to perfection. My old love for her returned and soon she came to live in my heart again as its sole resident, shattering in the process, my infatuation with the newer bike. But once I dropped any thoughts of (what had begun to feel like) infidelity, she got her revenge. She waited for the moment to come as it finally did when one hot summer afternoon, I was riding on a narrow mud road that snaked through a dense patch of forest not 30 kilometres from home, but far enough from any habitation. Suddenly, the piston developed an unexplained hiccup in its movement and for less than a minute, the engine sputtered and then lapsed into silence. The electrical system might have a loose contact, I thought, having no option but to stop and check the various places where such problems lurk. The battery was on full charge, the fuse was still valid and the spark plug was sparking; it all looked fine. But every time I tried the kick-start, the engine would sputter into brief life, as if tantalizing me with a bit of promise, before becoming still and unresponsive yet again. It was frustrating.

Not knowing what else to do, I sat on a nearby rock and looked at her. I felt myself slipping into surrender mode. I let my exasperation fade away and my affection for her surface in its place. I told her I was sorry. Then said it again. I could feel her thawing. And when, after a few more minutes of some diplomatic placation, I started her engine, she began purring away as if nothing at all had happened. She had forgiven me my transgression yet again.

Doesn't all this interaction with a mere machine suggest a hint of wackiness? I mean it's a machine after all and machines don't feel jealous for heaven's sake! It is absolutely impossible that a machine had planned its revenge and waited for the right moment to indulge in it. And to think of a machine as a beautiful woman. Surely that must classify as some exotic sexual aberration? 'Machinophilia', perhaps?

Over the years, I've taken cross-country rides but a decade and a half has gone by since the last long ride from Pune to the Himalayan foothills of Kumaon, when I'd had Meena as a pillion.

I decide to go for a ride to Goa and check out if I still have the ability for long-distance riding.

The Thwarted Pigs of Arambol

Two hours out of Pune, I am riding through the Taminhi Ghat singing old Hindi songs to myself. With a helmet on and the visor drawn, one can have a great private concert. The performer and the audience locked in symbiotic union. The voice reverberates within the inner confines of the helmet and comes through loud and clear.

Main zindagee ka saath nibhata chala gaya...
Har fikr ko dhuen mein udata chala gaya...
(I kept company with Life, blowing
away every worry in smoke)

The newly paved road all along the Sahyadri range makes for good riding and with just one brief stop for chai and a you-know-what, I make it to the Mumbai-Goa highway. A hundred kilometres done and only 240 more to go. The first stop being Ganpatipule, located

20 kilometres off the Mumbai-Goa highway, on the Ratnagiri coast.

Ganpatipule is a little seaside temple village, which is well known on the pilgrim route because of its large Ganesh temple built right on the beach. I walk into the lobby of Hotel Shreesagar – and am given a fairly decent room for a negotiated price of Rs. 300. After an hour of recovering from the ride, a bath and with cleaner clothes on, I take a leisurely walk through the one-street village. Night is setting in as I find myself keeping increasingly brisk pace with a youngish Brahmin who is on his *parikrama* of the temple. He looks splendid in his *dhoti* of red silk, which has been draped with special care. Each pleat has been folded and ironed to a sharp crease. Bright vermilion streaks vertically across his forehead like a meteor on fire.

With a *pooja-thali* in his hands and *shlokas* on his lips, he leads and I follow him all the way into the temple where resides the deity in full splendour. Ensconced on the left in a large niche sits the Elephant God Ganesha, adorned with ornaments and surrounded by his favourite *modak ladoos* which are heaped in plates and may become the *prasad* after the *pooja*. I look into the eyes of the five-foot-high idol and the Lord seems to stare right back at me. I imagine him smiling as if we have just shared a cosmic joke.

I pay my obeisance, then walk on to the beach making my way towards the darker part, where the lights of the temple fade and the stars become bright. The moon is on the rise and the gentle ocean waves sing a song of celestial welcome to another lovely night. Phosphorescence shimmers on the ocean like an emerald carpet. By 8 o'clock, the crowds have left and I can see no one on the beach. I sit cross-legged on the still warm sand and spend time taking fistfuls of it and letting the gritty grains trickle over my feet and calves. I spot waves of silver form a few hundred feet away from me and my eyes follow a single column of approaching froth to watch it burst into moon-soaked diamonds, which scatter on the beach.

The clock on my mobile says it's nearing midnight and I get up and walk back to my hotel. I realize I've not had any dinner and resolve to compensate with a good breakfast next morning.

The second day's ride begins early. While my omelette is being prepared, I consult the desk clerk at the hotel, who suggests I take the coastal road to Rajapur and join the Mumbai-Goa highway there. This will mean more time on the road but then, I'm not in any hurry either. I'm soon passing through some very picturesque scenery of ploughed red earth, of isolated coastal jungle villages with their contained lifestyles. Everywhere, even in the smaller places, I see prosperity and smiles. There are PCOs and Internet cafés and I'm getting a very strong signal on my mobile too. This is a new India I'm riding through. I cross three very scenic, fairly long, shining new bridges over creeks where fisherfolk mend their nets and take care of their boats before venturing out to reap the sea's bounty. It is a happy India I'm experiencing. Or is it that I myself am so happy that I see only happiness all around? Misery, like beauty, is also probably in the eyes of the beholder.

The day is getting warm and I shed my jacket, and then exchange my long sleeved, black shirt for a white T-shirt, and now this feels better. The helmet remains, mainly because of its visor, which offers welcome shade from the glare of the sun off the shining road. Soon I stop for lunch at a road side shack where the menu includes Goan fish curry and rice. I'm not too far from paradise.

As I pass the 'Welcome to Goa' signs, the world changes. The earth has turned bright brick red and the highway becomes broad and smooth. The Maharashtra section of NH-17 was just passable. In Goa, everything about it looks better maintained. It is no wonder that Goa was judged the best state in India.

At Pernem, I detour off towards my stop for the

night... Arambol beach. The narrow winding road takes me through border villages, which have a mixed-culture ambience. A mixture of Maharashtrian and Goan. Arambol is a hippietype village – what Anjuna used to be 20 years ago. Almost the entire tourist population in Arambol is European, Korean or Australian. I was the only Indian there. I saw ageing hippies and young hippies-in-the-making. I have long held a fantasy of riding my Enfield on the firm wet sand of a beach and to this end I make the first mistake of the trip. I ride on to the sand and immediately get stuck. The loaded Enfield is too heavy for this kind of thing. I had spoiled my clutch plates once, when I was similarly stuck on a sandy patch on a Himalayan road; but now that I'm a bit wiser, I cool off the accelerator and look for help with a plea on my face. Soon enough, the Nepali food shack manager who has been staring at me comes over and lifts the rear of the bike as I ease my weight off it to help it cross this mini Sahara.

I look for a place to stay. I ask my rescuer for suggestions and he directs me to a house nearby, which is really a few small thatched rooms fused together with no particular symmetry or pattern in mind. I ride down the slight depression in the road and park the bike under a large jackfruit tree, which stands in the corner of the patch of land in front of the house. Across, in another corner of the open space, an elderly woman is tearing up pieces of dry chapatis and tossing them to the two mongrels that frisk excitedly around her. A man, probably her husband, slinks his malnourished body into a darker corner of the covered porch.

She is a small-statured woman with the thin wiry body typical of those for whom physical labour is a way of life. A worn-out faded brown cotton sari is wrapped in the Konkani manner, with a part of the sari passing between her thighs and tucked at the base of her spine, just above her stringy buttocks. Her well-oiled hair, flashing in the sunlight, is tied behind in a skull-tight bun. Red and green glass bangles tinkle as she washes her hands and then comes over to where I am standing. Her mouth spreads in a taut smile when I tell her I'm looking for accommodation for one night.

She asks me if I am on my own, then leads me to the right side of the house, along a fence of an untended bush of duranta. There are two rooms of unplastered brick sharing a wall, each with three cemented steps leading up to an unshaded door. There is a stack of rotting branches heaped nearby. Mosquitoes hum me a welcome as she clicks open the lock on the door, struggles with the rusted iron latch and then stands aside for me to look into the room. It has no toilet of its own she says, but there is a pig-toilet at the back and when I look out of the open window, I see an orchard crowded with banana, coconut and betel nut trees; and two families of pigs clothed in dried muck, roaming happily all around.

'Shambhar rupayee,' she says without me asking.

Only a hundred rupees, but it's not to save money that I say yes to the lady of the house. There are two reasons. One being that I believe we should periodically put ourselves through some physical discomfort, even disgust, to better appreciate the good things we take for granted in our everyday privileged lives. The other reason was the face of the lady. She was a poor woman and the hundred rupees would mean a lot to her. I could read that in the expectancy on her face.

I didn't like the small rectangular room, which had a single window and dank walls. A naked light bulb stuck out from one of the walls. When I looked up at an old discoloured fan, which hung from a wooden rafter in the roof, she smiled and said *'Chaalat nahi'* (Doesn't work). Cobwebs adorned one corner of the ceiling and empty carcasses of a few unfortunate insects were testimony to the prowess of the plump spider that sat in the midst of his stringy secretions. The room had a metal bed, painted an appalling green with a stiff mattress which smelt like it hadn't been aired for quite a while. The silence was punctuated with grunts and squeals from the boisterous pigs. The smells around weren't exactly pleasing. It was the toilets visible from the open window that revolted me.

This 'hotel' sure was different from the Taj Intercontinental.

The lady was sensitive to my facial expressions and

must have realized I needed to be reassured. Inclining her head, she turned her eyeballs towards the backyard and gestured that I should follow her. She said she'd show me how these toilets function.

The pig-toilet is a Goan institution fast fading into oblivion. Essentially just an elevated brick platform over a hole in the ground, with a woven coconut frond curtain around it to provide some kind of privacy, this system of waste disposal is ingenious to the extreme. Using natural porcine tendencies to its advantage and cutting out the need for any other more complicated method, the pig-toilet also precludes the need to feed the pigs anything else. And if the smug, happy faces of the pigs are any indication, one could say that this is a system that works, give or take a mishap or two.

Every toilet comes equipped with a standard accessory – a thick four-feet-long wooden stick which one holds on to, not for support but as a weapon of defence. The lady picks up the stick and unabashedly shows me the technique for its use, much like an airhostess going through her preflight safety demonstration. I look on in horrified amazement. One delivers, she says, a sharp hit on the flat snout of the pig as soon as it gets too close to the flanks. Timing is everything. With almost motherly pride, she tells me her pigs are smart and they are quick! So I'll just have to be quicker, won't I? It is almost as if a challenge is being thrown. Who will win? The pig or the tourist?

Either outcome appears to be the same to her, although I suspect she is marginally partial to her pigs. Then as if embarrassed by her bias, and letting her voice adopt an insider's tone, she tells me not to get taken in by their delighted grunts. They can be quite dangerous. One German, an animal rights activist, in his kindness, had hesitated to hit them and had consequently to be rushed to the government hospital in Mapusa with a portion of his rear taken from him. 'My pigs are not polite like perhaps German pigs.' She laughs at her own joke. I admire her for that. A sense of humour even! Nevertheless, I decide to take a rain check on using her rustic restroom.

At the shack where the Nepali manager had helped me with my bike earlier in the evening, I have a light supper of vegetable noodles. I want to avoid going into the challenging toilet but an hour later I find I am back at the shack to eat some Goan fish curry and drink some of the local brew. The ride has made me hungrier than I had thought. The spicy curry-rice and the intoxicating cashew *feni* have somehow made me brave. I start to believe I can handle the pigs tomorrow; even teach them a lesson to keep their noses out of my business.

I need to stretch my legs and go out for a walk up

to Arambol beach. I see village youngsters playing cricket; then a little along the way, a group of Koreans practicing Tai-chi, looking very graceful, powerful and spiritual. I fall into conversation with a fortyish looking villager and when he learns that I've come on a motorcycle, he says, *'Hya vayaat?'* (At this age?), almost disapprovingly. Must be the white hair that camouflages this young heart but yes, I do look ancient. The body is 54 years old but the soul is ageless. Isn't that what the Vedas say? He himself has never ever strayed more than 30 kilometres from his village. He says this with a tinge of self-righteous pride. As if he's been more loyal. I then ask him his name and I lose a bet with myself when I learn it isn't Mr. Frog Wellwala.

Back in my room, I have little difficulty in falling into deep sleep. Somewhere on the fringes of my dreams, I see an overly large porcine face waiting with an expectant gleam in its eye. When morning comes, I try to put a mental plug on my own digestive system, praying it will hold until I reach a more manageable toilet. It does. As I leave my adventurous accommodation the nice lady waves me goodbye while her thwarted pigs look cheated.

I reach Candolim Beach and find a room which has a *balcao* facing the sea. More important, it has a modern toilet. Two days go by. I am toasted to a darker brown by the sun and the salty waters. I extend my stay for another day but it too fades into night and I ready myself for the return ride.

Saying goodbye to the beach is never easy. This proximity to the sea has been such a joyous aspect of these last four days: the glittering waters dancing to the fantastic batons of the sun's rays, the fishing boats coming in with their hauls, the tiny crabs scampering over the wet shore. The breeze… the invigorating breeze... has been my masseuse. But now it's time and I have to be on my way.

The crows must get to eat a lot around here because the seat, the tank and even one of the indicators of the motorcycle has been blessed with fairly copious amounts of bird droppings. I wet a rag and spend some time cleaning, then look up. The extending branches of the mango tree seem studded with the undersides of over twenty dark shapes and before one of them can drop yet another of its white and grey *prasadam*, I roll out the bike and park it away from the tree under a blue-pink sky.

As I sip a last cup of tea, I look at my friend of 16 years and thank her again for bringing me to this heavenly place. She has brought me here before and has also taken me to the foothills of the Himalayas once. But that was long, long ago and to a bike, blessed as it is with 'no-mind', it is only the present that matters.

And the present feeling is one of goodbye.

Some dark still lingers on in the morning air as the right leg kick-starts the 350 cc engine into its gentle boom-boom. The early morning is chilly with cold ocean breeze. As I finally get moving, home in Pune seems far, far away.

The ride through Sunday-morning Goa carries the aroma of freshly baked bread. Newly awakened faces, looking suitably pious, walking up to the church. It is too early for the petrol pumps to open and I realize with regret that it was a mistake to have procrastinated on that. Should have filled up last evening.

As I near Sawantwadi, I've still not decided which road I'm going to take. There are numerous options as to where one can cross the Sahyadri range and this time I take the advice of a passerby who suggests the Amboli ghat road. This turns out to be good counsel because the winding ghat road takes me through densely wooded hills with very little traffic. The road is studded with slightly raised blobs of crushed stone and tar which put a bit of bounce into the ride. Even potholes don't carry the same degree of 'hate-factor' when one is on an Enfield as when one is driving a four-wheeler. A 'pee-chai-smoke' stop beckons and then the road begins to wind upwards again.

The petrol situation doesn't look too good and is becoming an increasing concern. The mountain road has taken a toll on the mileage and I'm trying mental power to help the bike delay that moment when the reserve tank would need to be tapped. On the highway, the bike was delivering an astounding 44 kilometres to the litre but I can now be sure of only going a further 40 kilometres on the 1.25 litre reserve capacity. I observe the anxiety building up in my physiology but somewhere I am enjoying the uncertain possibility of being marooned in one of these remote jungle communities and never being rescued. Will I then marry the chieftain's daughter and become the *mukhiya* when I am old?

A pebble under the tyre jerks me out of this reverie as I remind myself that I am already older than my may-have-been father-in-law and in any case, there must now be very few places on this planet where one can realistically expect to be 'absolutely marooned' or offered any of the chieftain's nubile daughters! Behind all these mind-distraction games, I hear the speedometer yelling that 35 of those 40 kilometres are already over and trouble is brewing. So I blank out the chieftain and his sexy progeny. I don't even get time to miss her because I suddenly come upon Azra, which looks like a big and busy village and see a large orange logo heralding a petrol pump. My vehement *'bhar daalo'* (fill it up) takes the petrol-pump attendant by surprise. What enthusiastic customers. On a Sunday morning too!

Towards Nipani, on a narrow, but paved road

between golden fields, a farmer is waiting to cross with his two huge buffaloes. It almost seems that he waited for exactly the perfect moment to startle one of those huge beasts right into the path of my speeding beast. But 60 kilometres per hour is an easy speed to be able to use both brakes and still remain astride – this time, with my front wheel only two feet away from the almost inviting soft (but firm) butt of the 20 litres a day milk machine.

I smile at (instead of curse) the farmer with a 'didn't get me this time' gleam in my eyes but he can't see my eyes, or my face, or the white hair – tucked under the helmet as I am. Probably mistook me for a young ruffian out to destroy his capital investment.

I am already crossing Karad with Kolhapur 40 kilometres behind me and it's only 2 p.m. by my mobile phone clock.

Gradually the possibility of reaching Pune that very evening grows distinct. The way the road is looking, with me comfortably touching 80 kilometres per hour, I might just be able to sleep in my own bed tonight.

At one point that afternoon, I become part of a dream sequence. Just ahead of me are three new Enfields with three sparkling, white-clad, prosperous looking farmers riding abreast across the wide highway. They are going at a uniform 70 with me overtaking them on the extreme right at a steady 80 kilometres per hour.

Four Enfields singing in unison and celebrating life with a thump and a vroooom…

Some more 'pee-chai-smoke' stops and a few hours later, I reach home. What follows is a reward… a hot bath coupled with her ministrations and with some Old Monk thrown in, lovely food and some great sleep. My snoring that night had a deep dugh… dugh… beat she tells me at dawn. But I know she's only pulling my leg.

To Goa and back is 1,000 kilometres from Pune. The fact that I've been able to ride this distance so comfortably has resulted in a surge of self-confidence.

I am now itching to go a much longer distance. Somewhere north? May be all the way into the Himalayas? The very thought of the Enfield sweeping along those high curvaceous roads is thrilling. I can already smell the deodars.

Gradually an idea begins to hatch. 'Go Ladakh,' the hatchling whispers, as yet innocent of grammar.

Getting Ready

I begin to plan out a one month vacation from work. My clinic appointments will need to be rescheduled. I surf the net, looking for information from others who had travelled the route on motorcycles. I learn that the Manali-Leh road opens only between late May and early November every year. It is also 475 kilometres of the roughest terrain in the country with the road going over mountain passes as high as 5,660 metres.

Every day I tick off one entry or two from my list of things to do. The list has been divided into sections.

1. Toning up the body : I begin a daily physical exercise routine, which includes 12 kilometres of cycling and 30 minutes at the Pune University gym.
2. Getting the motorcycle ready : Not being particularly clever with the mechanics of motorcycles, I begin

spending some hours at the workshop where Ramesh instructs me on basic, on-the-road emergency maintenance. Like most motorcycle mechanics in India, Ramesh is a self-taught, hands-on guy who shows me how easy it was to replace snapped brake, accelerator or clutch cables. Together we install the new electronic timing device which makes setting the points redundant. Even the fairly involved process of changing worn out clutch plates now looks like a task I can handle if I needed to. I also learn how to replace a punctured tube. My spares include two extra tubes and a special lever needed to snap the tyre off the wheel rim. I buy a new foot pump. Other spares include a spark plug, ignition coil, rectifier and two 15-amp fuses.

3. Collecting the things I would need on the road includes clothes appropriate for the various temperature zones I would pass through. From T-shirts for the blazing summer of the plains to a high-altitude jacket for the icy cold weather of the high Himalayas.

I assemble a first aid kit including tablets for high altitude sickness, stomach upsets, pain, and creams for skin rash and muscle strain.

Other items include a digital camera, Swiss knife,

a needle with thread, a coil of thin nylon rope and a hip flask. A blank notebook, a pen and a pencil. A tiny screw driver for the frame of my eyeglasses.

I connect with a group of four bikers who are also planning to ride from New Delhi to Leh (Ladakh). I join the group and we all begin to plan our trip through emails on a message board. The plan is for the five of us to meet in New Delhi on June 22nd and ride together to Leh and then on to Srinagar and finally Jammu, from where we would go our separate ways. Since I am coming by road all the way, my date of departure from Pune is to be June 10th.

(By a series of coincidences, the plan did not work for me. Except for the one time when we all rode together for a few kilometres from Manali to near Rohtang La, I found myself riding alone throughout the trip. It was almost as if I had to do this journey on my own.)

Riding with a group provides tremendous support to each member and the advantages are obvious. Aside from being mentally assured that help is available in case of accident or mechanical malfunctions, a group provides evenings full of entertainment. Songs, humour and good company can do wonders for the fatigued body after a hard day's ride and I missed out on that. There were some advantages to riding alone too. And these revealed themselves in subtle and mysterious ways.

Riding alone, one can think in the singular. One doesn't have to think conventional thoughts. Travelling with company, one inevitably succumbs to group-thinkism, always conscious of being accountable to the group and in return, expecting similar accountability. A group is a life-support system.

Maybe that is what I'm running away from: my insured lifestyle in Pune where everyday, I go to bed feeling safe and wake up feeling secure.

My various check-lists have been attended to. It is the 9th of June, 2004. Tomorrow I leave.

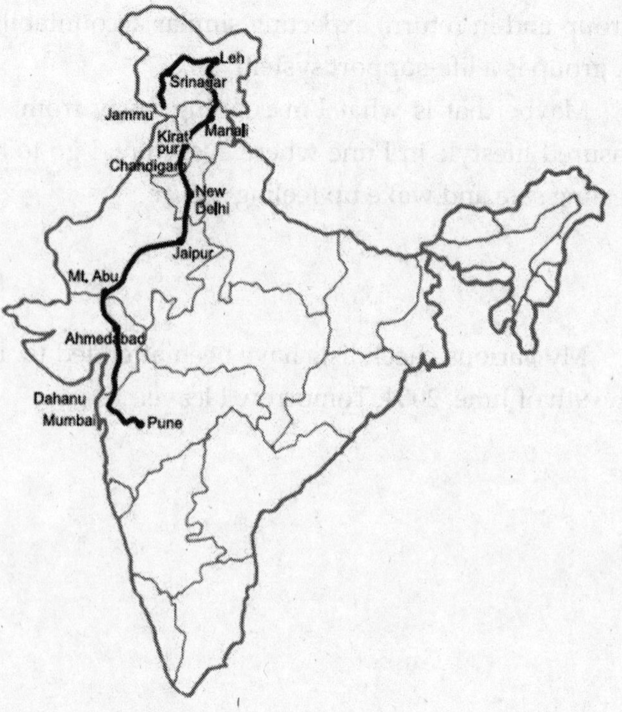

Route Map of the 4300 kms motorcycle journey from Pune with halts at Dahanu, Ahmedabad, Mt. Abu, Jaipur, New Delhi, Kiratpur, Kasol, Manali, Darcha, Pang, Leh, Hunder, Leh, Dras, Srinagar, Patnitop and Jammu.

Come to the edge.

We can't.

We're afraid.

Come to the edge.

We can't.

We will fall!

Come to the edge.

And they came.

And he pushed them.

And they flew.

Guillaume Apollinaire,

1880-1918

French poet, philosopher

Martial Law for a Motorcyclist

It has rained the night before and the morning air retains a degree of chill. Sunrise in Pune is still an hour away. A faint wisp of mist all around limits visibility but that's really no bother since traffic is sparse this early in the morning, with only the occasional car hurrying away towards Mumbai, lost to sight in less than half a minute.

I open the visor of my helmet to welcome the feel of cold breeze on my face but in the bargain also have to contend with the loud gushing sound that accompanies it. That doesn't feel good, so I pull down my curtain of Plexiglas to enclose myself again in my capsule-like helmet cutting off noise and letting exhaled air, circulating in an enclosed space, warm my face. The dark sunscreen of the visor tints everything around me in a cloak of grey-blue. New buildings looking like boxes of blue glass sprouting on a lawn of grey concrete dominate the landscape on either side of the highway. I am just out of Pune, headed northwest on National Highway 4 (NH-4) passing through a suburb in the making.

Roads are being laid. Yellow and red excavators and bulldozers appear crouched and waiting, as if anxious for another day of hectic activity. One of the big machines, its hood open, is being revved up by a grease-smudged young man. Where not too long ago, the ears heard the tinkling of bells as oxen helped plough the farmland; it is now the reign of the internal combustion engine.

The past is literally being bulldozed away. And the trucks cart away more than just old bricks, broken chunks of cement and warped rods of rusted steel. If you looked closely you would also see bits of songs and pieces of folkdances crumpled within this rubble; torn pages of history which no one wants to read today.

Going… going… gone.

A fast moving bright blue Volvo bus is overtaking me on my right and abruptly my focus shifts to the NOW.

These early minutes of the ride are a period of adjustments. Taking a firmer grip of the handle, slowing down a bit, I stand on the foot-rests and let the trousers settle to their natural fall. The thin chamois leather gloves take their time fitting comfortably over my fingers. These gloves are old and shaded dark with patches of dried grease and sweat accumulated over previous rides. I have a brand new pair tucked somewhere in one of the saddle-bags, but they are thickly lined with down and I will need them only when I approach the cold Himalayan ranges.

A checklist unfolds in the brain – a motorcyclist's version of a pre-flight check.

One cluster of thoughts monitors the overall health of the motorcycle and remains alert to any sign of deviation from its current peak mechanical condition. I am glad I opted for the streamlined saddle-bags which have been loaded and checked for balance on a sample ride the previous evening. The heavier spares and tools have been divided and packed for easier accessibility. On the highway, you don't want to open up the entire bag because the small spanner you need to tighten the brakes is inconveniently packed. The mechanic in me is processing a variety of other inputs. Do the tyres maintain the correct amount of spring in their step? Are the clutch and accelerator cables gliding smoothly in their casings? Do the brakes feel right? Are the tappets still on friendly terms with the actions of the piston? It is too early in the ride for things to start going wrong with the motorcycle and such monitoring will gain importance only as the miles add on. All questions answered for now, these motorcycle-connected thoughts fade from centre stage to be replaced by another cluster, which is focused on rider-status.

Is the body sitting in natural alignment? Are the muscles of the forearms holding the handle with more than necessary effort? Are the ankles and feet too tensed? Are the eyes squinting without reason? Is the forehead unnecessarily creased? It's going to be a long ride and tiny muscular stresses can build up over a period of time to become major points of contention. The heart, at its own 72 beats a minute cannot, at first, keep pace with the much faster beat of the engine, but I try out a variety of mental calibrations and soon the equation is adjusted to read: One heart beat = four engine beats. There... the 'dugh... dugh... dugh... dugh' of the four-stroke engine is now also the beat my body is synchronized to.

Now that that's all set, I can forget about my body. Just water it, feed it and rest it and it should be fine. I don't have to get too involved in 'body-gossip'. To this end, I have delegated all body duties; so each organ can take care of itself as well as cooperate with its colleagues. No complaints or pleas for help will be entertained, be they from exhausted muscle groups, finicky taste buds or sore eyes. Sometimes such martial law announcements are required to keep all the millions of cells that constitute this miracle of a body functioning in some sort of physiological harmony. I cannot have mutiny on board.

But neither will I push my subjects to the limits of their endurance. I am a benevolent, loving dictator. (Doesn't every dictator think that?) I will rest frequently. Every 50 minutes or so, I will stop to rehydrate the body machine. Water is an elixir that I carry in adequate supply.

Other fundamental commandments have been agreed upon. I will ride only in daylight and will let the progress of the day's ride decide where I will sleep for the night. Also, I have promised Meena I will not litter.

I'm approaching a junction where this new bypass that I've been riding on joins with the old highway.

An octroi check post on my left wears its usual garland of loaded trucks with their spillage of drivers waiting their turn. One of the drivers has his face covered in white foam and is using the large rear view mirror of his truck to shave. Young boys dart between the trucks, some ferrying glasses of hot *chai*, others selling newspapers or cigarettes. This place is organized to wait. I ride through the melee at snail's pace. I can hear a radio asking everyone an easy question: '*Choli ke peeche kya hai*?' But it's too early in the morning for that sort of thing. Or is it?

The human brain is really a radio, receiving thought waves from source stations it is tuned to. Turn the frequency-selecting dial to Radio Misery or Radio Bliss or Radio Sex (which plagiarizes programmes from the previous two) and that will be the content of the thought programme we will receive.

My own radio receiver has just received a broadcast from the official Radio Cosmic Law (RCL-FM). The announcer is declaring that a new legislation is now replacing all previous laws. Everyone was now allowed to bliss-out. It is official! The Creator encourages everyone to be happy. Enjoy life today and all other days too. And even after the body material drops dead and we return to becoming conscious of our true nature, back to being the conscious souls we really always are, this enjoyment can continue.

The law, the RJ says, allows us to opt for a state of perennial joy. And with no payments to be made, it is a bargain deal. No guilt to feel. Be as joyous as you want to be. There is only one condition here, the announcer cautions. Your happiness – it can't be at anyone else's cost. Heavy karmic penalties are laid out for those transgressing this rule and it is only the absolutely stupid who would break it. With happiness so easily and freely available, only an idiot would go about acquiring it with a greedy material-grabber's mindset that wants everything for itself, regardless of what it costs others. As a consequence, this insatiable mind develops the fear of losing what it has unethically grabbed. Stress is then its karmic penalty.

So yes, we are really radios that can tune in and out of the zillions of thought-transmitting radio stations.

Even Radio Crazy.

I am meandering along at around 50 kilometres per hour through an area before the Western Ghats begin. The scenery is acquiring a picturesque quality.

These hills are densely forested with steep slopes that make it ideal for silvery white rainwater to cascade and leap downward towards the gradually swelling rain river below. The valleys are verdant green, with a touch of vibrant orange contributed by the flowering Pangara trees.

The day has started to warm up. The old tar highway intermittently flashes brilliance when its broken stone edges catch the slanting rays of the rising sun.

Another four hours of riding takes me through the industrial townships of Panvel and Taloja before I come to the newly constructed highway that allows me to bypass Thane and get on to Godbunder road to take me on to NH-8.

At Charoti Naka, I get off the highway and turn westward towards the sea. Groves of tall palms line both sides of the road and the sun, playing hide-and-seek behind them, highlights me in strobe. I am approaching Dahanu, which is to be my halt for the night.

Dahanu seems to be trapped between two worlds. Only three hours away is the bustling metropolis of big-city Mumbai and Dahanu cannot remain immune to its influence. With faster trains and better roads, Dahanu now takes pride in calling itself a suburb of Mumbai. At least, that's what the real estate brochures say.

With the Mannor forest on its east and the Arabian Sea to its west, Dahanu also has a sizable tribal population. I pass through a crowded market where colourfully decked Adivasi women with baskets full of *chickoos* vie with each other for the attention of their customers. Boisterous fisherwomen who have platters of fresh fish to sell, contribute to the din. Brilliant white teeth framed in sunburnt black faces reflect the light from the early evening sun. There is a vibrant energy in the air. What is it that makes laughing so easy for these women? Surely they have their poverty and alcoholic husbands to contend with? Food to cook, children to take care of and their businesses to run? None of them looks tired.

Alone on the bike, away from routine restrictions, I feel different. No one on the road knows anything about me. I am free of my personal history and can be whoever I want to be. I can even change my personality as often as I change my shirt. Through Gujarat, I can be a philosophising old man. In Rajasthan, I'll change into a happy, smiling joker and in Punjab, I might turn into a romantic.

All through these metamorphoses, I have to be careful I don't get knocked off the road by any of those recklessly driven trucks and turn into a statistic!

The old road is beginning to narrow in patches before opening up again and I have to put a pause on my mental wanderings and concentrate on the riding.

Soon I am in small town Dahanu.

Be Here Now in Dahanu

My elder sister and her husband, both doctors, have been here for over two decades and it is not difficult for me to locate their new hospital, a large building with their residence perched on the topmost floor.

I am expected and welcomed by a pert young nurse and a bewildered looking ward boy. I park, unload and climb up the broad stairs with the boy dragging up my unwieldy, bulging saddle-bags.

With only a glance at my face, my brother-inlaw rushes to open the two bottles of beer he has kept chilled and ready for this very moment. I take mine into the bathroom and the drink cools me from inside while the shower and soap clean the body's external wrapping.

Comfort. How addicted I am to you.

I lie down on the spare bed that has a side table on which stands a 1940s sepia picture of my parents, both looking very young, as if barely out of teenage. The photograph must have been taken in Karachi, a city they were soon forced to leave in the aftermath of Partition. I've seen this picture a long time ago. Today, it holds my attention as it has not done before. I stare at their eyes and through them enter into their minds; these two youngsters who were to become my father and my mother a decade later, but didn't know it then.

My sister returns from the mission hospital looking her usual capable self. She has always had a no-nonsense air about her. How often had my father asked me why I wasn't as responsible, studious, hardworking (and many other such qualities) as her. She's just helped deliver a baby girl and 'both mother and child are normal' is her reassuring pronouncement when her husband enquires how it all went.

As the three of us sit on the balcony overlooking Dahanu's main street, they ask about the route I've planned to take and I show it to them on the map. I can't tell if it is appreciation, amazement, or doubt that is in their thoughts as they wonder aloud about where I would sleep and how I would manage if 'something went wrong'. With a lifetime spent in encounters with birth, death and all the myriad problems that plague the human body in between these two events, they are only too aware of the various threats to my health that the journey might entail.

'Don't forget you are no longer young,' says my practical-minded sister.

Later in the evening, as I walk past the now almost empty marketplace in Dahanu, I see a prosperous but worried looking shopkeeper scowl at a young tribal girl who wants to buy just a bit of oil to cook her family's evening meal. She extends the small open bottle she has brought for it towards the plump shopkeeper who gestures for her to put it on the counter. She is smiling while he looks impatient, stressed and insecure.

Towards the beach the road becomes quiet and dark, and takes on an aura of mystery. The streetlights are few and far between and with their limited circle of influence, succeed more as milestones that mark the direction of this narrowing road. The roar of the sea is subdued and I can hear someone singing. A couple of naked light bulbs beckon me to what looks like a toddy shack. Country bar it is, and doing good business this evening. With around a dozen men being served the palm brew in earthen pots by a pair of young boys who are being kept on their feet, what with the barrage of frequent new orders from the progressively inebriated clientele. The relaxing *kolis* (fishermen) are singing what sounds like a naughty song because everyone around them is grinning. There is ribaldry in the air.

The singers are sitting a distance away on the sand within sight of the beach and I walk over to sit alone, a few yards from them. Service is five-star here because within minutes and even without asking, I am served with my own two litre jar of the white brew, an empty glass of uncertain lineage and a fistful of roasted green *harbara* which frolic with a life of their own on a patch of banana leaf.

The sea glimmers silver in the background.

Without meaning to, I become focused on my breathing. I slip into the role of an observer and feel my breath as it moves out of my nostrils and plays around that area where my moustache would be if I'd had one. Just like they taught me at the Vipasana Centre in Igatpuri.

Diary Entry: Vipasana International Academy

The road to Igatpuri is not a particularly long one – just about seven hours from Pune – but it has taken me two years to travel it. I've finally taken the plunge and keeping all apprehensions on hold, I have committed to being locked up in an institution for ten days. Everyone who has been here has warned me that the rules are rigid. They wake you up at 4 a.m., put you through a rigorous schedule right up till 9:30 p.m. They feed you only one-and-

a-half simple meals a day and compel you to exist in tiny Spartan cubby holes, which most times are shared with one or two other 'inmates'. And you can't complain because absolutely no talk is allowed for the first nine days. They call it 'Noble Silence'. Welcome to the Vipasana International Academy (VIA), where, like the guys in 'Hotel California', you may enter but you cannot leave. Not for ten days.

Nestled in a picturesque location in Igatpuri far from habitation, the VIA is an austere place. But the atmosphere the evening I arrive is festive enough. Registration is in progress amidst a torrential downpour. Despite almost 400 new entrants, there is no confusion in the hall. They're well-organized.

At 7 p.m., the orientation starts. The large dining hall suddenly looks small as over 300 males are cramped in, and a dour-looking man with a graveyard manner begins his welcome speech without even a trace of a smile. He is the course manager. It's going to be no picnic, he warns us, and goes on to detail all restrictions and rules to be followed while we are on campus. He alternates between Hindi and English (there are a few foreigners amongst us) and ends with a one-time offer. Anyone with any doubts can leave right away – because after the clock strikes 8 p.m., no one will be allowed to drop out. None in the audience gets up to go.

Everyone is assigned their rooms, their laundry bags, etc. Money and valuables are to be put in storage until the end of the course. No reading or writing material is allowed and of course, no cigarettes or any other intoxicants.

I am inmate number 321 and my cell is G-3. I trudge towards it expecting the worst but I am in for a pleasant surprise. I have a room to myself and it has a bathroom attached. The guys in F-block are cramped two to a room, seven feet by six feet in size. Toilets for them are outside. There are also dorms with 18 to a room. Males and females are strictly segregated. Eye contact is discouraged.

By the end of the next afternoon, I have begun to regret my rejection of the introductory offer. I haven't enjoyed the first full day of Vipasana at all. The initial excitement of a spiritual quest has quickly vanished. I've been awake since 4 a.m. Around ten hours have been spent in sitting cross-legged, listening to a audio-tape that keeps repeating the first step in learning the technique of Vipasana meditation.

'Just concentrate on your respiration within the triangular area formed between the upper lip and the nostrils'. 'Observe. Just observe your breath as it travels in and out through your nostrils,''And don't try and alter your natural breathing pattern.'

'Just become aware'.

It had been initially exciting to think about nothing other than my breath, but after a while it became a bit dull and I had gone off on a high-speed thinking spree.

It is indeed difficult to silence the ongoing internal chatter with which the mind is constantly involved. Soon the pain in my legs took precedence over all other concerns. I felt growing cramps in both thighs. A portion of my spine had become painful too. Each minute had seemed excruciatingly long as I anxiously waited for the hourly meditation period to end. A five-minute break to stretch legs and then the tape: 'Begin again. Focus on your breath. Maintain perfect awareness. Try not to move at all, etc. etc.'

Between 7 and 8:30 p.m., is videotape discourse time. Meet Shri S. N. Goenka, the initiator of the Vipasana technique of meditation in modern times. He looked around 65 years old. He was not dressed in spectacular robes, nor does he have matted hair or an ash-smeared forehead. In fact, he looked exactly like what he really was – a retired businessman who has done it all and seen it all. Born in Burma (now Myanmar) to a rich family with international business connections, he was drawn towards Vipasana when nothing else worked to alleviate the intense chronic migraine headaches he was prone to in those early years. Where Swiss and American doctors offered only morphine as a pain reliever but no cure, the regular practice of Vipasana brought him freedom from his migraines and 'much much more than I had expected,' he says.

For 14 years Shri Goenka took training in this technique from Sayaji U Ba Khin of Burma, a master who wished that the technique of Vipasana would return to the land of its origin – India.

Shri Goenka began his video talk by telling us that Vipasana means seeing things as they are. Seeing their true nature. It is a technique of self-observation, truth observation, self-exploration and self-purification. It involves focusing on gross and subtle bodily sensations, learning to adopt sakshi bhav (an observer's stance) towards our physical and mental mechanisms.

Days two and three are exactly the same as day one. Same instructions on tape all day long (only the evening discourses are different) and I'm just about ready to climb the walls of my little cell as I turn in at night. I am hungry, bored and starved for company as I try to sleep on my thinly mattressed stone bed. I don't have writing material so I take the burnt wick of a candle and make seven vertical lines on the wall to record the number of days to go before release. I can rub one line off every night.

That is my only reward for another day of torture suffered. Sceptical and cornered as I feel, I have begun to notice a change in my dreaming pattern during the short six hours of sleep. I begin to have very vivid dreams and when the hated bell tinkles me into unwilling awakening at 4 a.m. every morning, I can remember each dream in detail. This hasn't happened to me in a long time. The dreams all have a scary Roald Dahlish quality about them. In one, my face has fallen off and keeps following me as I walk in a dark, lonely park. I look at my reflection in a pond and can see only a black void where my face should have been! I wake up sweating and then cannot go back to sleep. The watch shows 3:05 a.m. As I drink some water and go out for a breather, a large bat flutters uncomfortably close and I'm back into the room, resigned now to the fact that there's going to be no way out other than to suffer this through.

The next five days get surprisingly better. I've begun to get into the technique and have been experiencing an enhanced level of awareness and equanimity. The pain in my body is forgotten and I'm no longer in my 'complaining' mode. The technique is working. The daily meetings with my counsellor have helped give a personalized touch to the exercise. Each student is encouraged to discuss difficulties faced and the calm and caring approach of the counsellor is comforting and very educative. He cautions me from becoming exhilarated at the very pleasurable sensations I've been experiencing. 'Handle pain and pleasure with the same non-involved equanimity,' he urges. 'Everything will pass. Every emotion is temporary. Nature works on the Law of Impermanence – Anichya... Anichya... Anichya.'

By day eight, I'm glad I came here. I've begun thinking of Shri Goenka as Guruji now. Although he is not personally present, he seems real and alive. He lacks the charisma of Satya Sai Baba or the glamour of Osho, but Guruji's straight-forward, even somewhat dry manner, has an appealing quality of honesty about it.

Day nine 10 a.m. is the last hour of 'Noble Silence' but I'm no longer anxious to break into speech. It's been rather soothing to be quiet.

How often have I heard about the power of NOW. Spiritual leaders and new-age gurus daily extol the virtues of living in the 'present'. The *Sunday Times* can't print enough about it. These writings never fail to charge my resolve to implement the proffered advice but I can achieve this state of awareness only occasionally and then, only for a minute or so before the Non-Now reasserts its hold on the psyche.

Sitting on the beach in Dahanu that night, I become

aware that I am in the NOW. It is the moment where only the present matters.

Magic happens. The ever-buzzing internal dialogue dissolves in the sea of intensifying silence. Reactions and judgments, loves and hates, memories and regrets, desires and schemes seeking to satisfy them, and all the myriad thoughts that run amuck in the mind; all fade and dissolve into nothingness. Everything is blissfully quiet. Everything is glowing. Even stones have an aura of light emanating from them.

The world becomes bathed with a serene luminosity. No, the world is ever aglow with this bliss. It is only I, the observer, who has briefly opened his eyes to the ever-present reality of his essential self.

The first day's ride fades away into the past and doesn't exist anymore. The past and the future are a blank screen. It is the sound of the sea that fills my consciousness. Relieved of the memory of the day's events, my mind and my muscles seem to have forgotten their reasons for being tired. The 300 kilometres I've come on the first day are not even a thought. A sense of well-being engulfs me. It's been a therapeutic evening. Mind and body aided by the catalytic benevolence of two litres of the heady *som ras*, I forget my past even as I try to remember the way back to my lodging for the night.

Six Words are Enough

Early on the second day, I retrace the 24 kilometres I've detoured from the interstate highway and for another 100 kilometres, enjoy a pleasant enough ride. The highway is coursing its way over hill and dale and the terrain is spread wide open on both sides of the road.

It was too early to eat when I left Dahanu but now, after three hours of riding, I can feel a rumble from inside my stomach. The body is asking for some food. I find fulfilment for its needs at a roadside *dhaba* where the breakfast is piping hot *aloo-parathas*, preceded and followed by cups of *masala chai*.

Back on the road, I begin to notice a change of scene as I come to the chemical-industrial towns of Gujarat where the river Narmada begins to break down into a delta carrying effluent waste of vivid colours into the Arabian Sea. It is apocalyptic with plumes of thick black smoke whirling up towards the sky, finally mushrooming into a cloud of carbon which then showers down on the populace. This is an intensely industrialized belt as the highway takes me, first towards Vadodara and then on to my destination of the day – the textile city of Ahmedabad.

The highway is dotted with toll booths but in India, I've discovered, two-wheelers do not have to pay toll. I like that. The laws of this country are generous to the poor.

At one such tollbooth where, in spite of not having to pay toll, I still have to pass through the gates where other cars and trucks awaited their turn, I suddenly find myself being nudged off the channel into the cement embankment on my right. A white car is crowding me, not allowing me the few inches of space I need.

'*Arre saale*' the driver's yell is loud enough even through my helmet.

Preventing a small collision, I regain my balance and look at my tormentor. Maybe it is the smallness of their car that made them seem to fill it up, but I see a grossly fat couple inside, both about 40 years old.

'*Abbe gaddhey, marna hai kya*?' (Hey you donkey. Want to Die?).

I say nothing but the fat man isn't ready to give up.

'*Kyon bey? Sunta nahi kya*?' (Why? Can't you hear?), he challenges me again.

I think he is only trying to impress his wife, who is smiling appreciatively at her brave spouse.

I decide to try something. The Enfield is also a motorcycle much favoured by the police and the military and I have been often mistaken for a senior officer of these two services.

Looking at him steadily, I open the visor of my helmet and notice his surprise as he sees my ancient face. Then, in a soft, non-threatening tone, deliver my threat. I simply ask him if he has ever been beaten by an army man.

'*Fauji se kabhi maar khaya hai*?' as if it was something he had missed in life; something I could well deliver. His expression changes as if a switch had been flicked. He stops speaking. His overflowing wife has also assumed a tense expression on her ample face. The man is now in an abnormal hurry to move. He looks straight ahead and takes off a bit too fast for the ten rather big rumble strips ahead.

Six words can be a potent force. It's the tone that is important here. Being a speech therapist has its advantages!

A green signboard on the highway informs me that Ahmedabad is only 50 kilometres away.

Think about Ahmedabad and I can't but think about the recent communal riots. As a child of refugee parents who had to survive in the aftermath of the country's violent partition, I am no stranger to the results of communal discord. Uprooted families rebuilding shattered lives, feeling hated and hating in return, broiling in memories of fearful nights when they had to barricade themselves behind suddenly flimsy looking doors, terrified that the burning torch or the sharpened sword would soon decide their own fate. Every such story my mother told me came alive with frightening vividity.

My mother came from an affluent doctor's family. Her father, with his medical education from the Grant Medical College, Mumbai, in the early 1900s, had prospered doctoring the *nawabs* of Larkana, Sindh. My mother had many stories to tell of the extravagant gifts that followed each home visit my *nana* made. The *nawabs* paid in trunks full of clothes and baskets of fruit.

One of mother's stories:

She was 16 years old when this happened. They had just moved into the new house that her father had built in Larkana. She remembers it was coloured white and had a dome and a basement where she played with her friends. Late one night, there was a loud knocking on the door, which got the entire household out of bed. This is how she told the story:

Your nana unlatched the door. Four burly Pathans

stood beyond the threshold. To my young mind, the big men, clad in dark salwaarkurtas, standing in the faintly lighted porch, were an intimidating sight. What scared me were the daggers strapped around their waists and the very long-barrelled guns in their hands. The turbaned one, who appeared to be their leader, was Vazir Sonu Khan, and said he had a message from his master Nawab Gaibi Khan.

Gaibi Khan, who was then lord of Gaibi dera, a village about 40 kilometres from Larkana, wanted the daaktar to be quickly summoned to save the apple-of-his-eye, his six-year-old grandson Ahmed Sultan, who had suddenly taken very ill and was now writhing in pain. It was an emergency and would the respected daaktar please hurry. The driver of the nawab's car had not even switched off the engine, but Dada was not to be rushed. He asked Sonu Khan to describe the child's symptoms and then packed his bag with everything he would need. They left and we didn't see Dada for seven days. There were no telephones then, not in Gaibi dera. We had no way of knowing what had happened. Zamindars were like absolute monarchs in their fiefdoms. Had the boy died? Were they blaming my father? Where was he? Seven days later he came back in a large car, one of the Nawab's prized possessions. Two large metal trunks were unloaded from the rear of the car by the same four men who had come to fetch him the week before. There was also a huge degchi, which we were told contained cooked venison.

'Dada, what happened?' I asked as soon as he had a wash and a cup of tea.

'Oh… everything was fine,' he had replied.

'Dada… I want to know what happened right from when you drove off that night,' I had pestered him.

He said they had reached Gaibi dera at 2 a.m. Roads were narrow and rough and they had taken two hours to cover the distance.

The old nawab was waiting for them. He was a big man even by Pathan standards. He wore a white kaftaan and his salwaars were reputed to be made from nine yards of poplin latha. And his hair and beard were dyed red with henna. Known to treat both his Hindu and Muslim 'subjects' with equal justice, the nawab was respected for his fairness.

At any other time, it would be his warm broad smile with which he greeted his visitors, but that night his face was grim. 'Daaktar, save my grandson,' were the only words he spoke as he led Dada towards the child's room. Dada said that the boy, who was lying on a large bed surrounded by his mother and three other women, was in obvious pain which seemed to be spasmodic, occurring at intervals of about two minutes. The child was clutching his stomach and crying. Dada said it was a simple case of a severely constipated digestive tract. The boy had not passed stools for four days but had continued to eat, causing a kind of traffic jam.

Dada said he had administered an enema and retired to the room they had allotted him in the guesthouse which was in a separate building. Early next morning he was awakened by an old woman who said the nawab wanted to see him. Gaibi Khan was waiting near the door of his haveli. Ahmed

Sultan was going to be all right. A miraculous recovery had occurred.

Awash with relief, the nawab was grateful beyond words. He wouldn't hear of letting Dada go back to Larkana so soon, wanting him to supervise the child's recuperation. A majlis to celebrate his grandson's return to good health was planned and Dada was the guest of honour.

Much later, when the partition of the country became a certainty and Hindus began to leave Larkana, Gaibi Khan sent Sonu Khan and four armed men to safely escort our family to Karachi. Even train journeys were becoming dangerous with frequent reports of passengers being massacred. The Pathans came with us on the train from Larkana. They kept watch as we stayed in Gaibi Khan's house in Karachi for the four days it took to finalise travel arrangements. The Pathans booked our seats on the ship to Bombay, escorted us to the docks and left only after making sure we were safe. This story, however, did not have a completely happy ending. We heard later that Gaibi Khan had been arrested because he was sympathetic to the plight of Hindus and had helped many escape the wrath of the marauding killer gangs. Those were times when tempers ran high on both sides of the religious divide. The Khan was seen as a traitor and a sentence of prolonged imprisonment was passed. But this prisoner was never imprisoned. The Khan, unable to take the fact of his sentence, had a heart attack when he was being taken to Sukkhur Jail and was dead before he entered it.

I enter the city of Ahmedabad and wend my way through crowded streets towards the cantonment area where I am to meet Dr. Major Dinesh Kumar who is a friend of a friend and has offered to put me up for the two days I plan to stay in Ahmedabad. We make contact on the phone and I am instructed to wait at the Rajasthan Hospital crossing and look out for a green Fiat Uno. I am glad to get off the bike and stretch my stiff legs. I am particularly happy to take off the uncomfortable helmet. In the heat of the blazing city, I have been sweating under the claustrophobic confines of my head armour.

Presently the doctor arrives in his Fiat, and signals for me to follow him. We ride through a maze of military buildings to reach his residential quarters. As the Major gets out of the car, I see he is around 35 years old, wiry thin and very crisp in his movements. He looks very smart in his uniform. In formal army manner, he gestures for me to follow him. I can see that he looks upon hosting me as an obligation he is fulfilling for our common friend and I decide to try and make it as painless for him as I can.

His apartment is on the ground floor and has the look of a bachelor pad. Clothes strewn over chairs, books on the sofa and an ashtray full of cigarette butts. I am glad to rest my fatigued body on a cane chair in the balcony while he busies himself with making tea. I am happy to sit alone on something that doesn't move. The apartment is stiflingly hot and I want to take off even my thin shirt but I don't know my host well enough yet to take such a liberty. Dinesh, when he brings out the two cups of tea, tells me he is a psychiatrist. His wife has gone to her parents' home in Kerala to deliver their first child and he is on his own for a few months. Must be an exciting time for him, the fact of soon becoming a father, I say. He smiles, looks at his watch and says he has to go back to the hospital to finish his working day.

'More patients?' I ask him. Psychiatrists must be busy considering the number of soldiers who succumb to the stress of a posting, particularly in J&K. But the doctor's answer surprises me.

'Canteen stores duty,' he says, explaining that every officer is assigned additional duties on a rotational basis and this month he was responsible for the canteen. He rushes off and I quickly get out of my sticky sweaty clothes and head for the shower. Dinesh returns around 8 p.m. and we go out for dinner at a nearby restaurant and then it's early to bed.

As I sleep under the whirling ceiling fan in my room that night, I try and re-enter that magical world of 'NOW' by emptying my mind of all thought, but it is not going to work. Not tonight. Must be the heat. Or maybe the fat man at the tollnaka had something to do with it. I want to get out of Ahmedabad. I had planned to stay for two days but now I've changed my mind. I resolve to leave early in the morning, detour off my planned route (which was to take me straight to Jaipur), and spend a day in the cooler environs of Mt. Abu which is on the Rajasthan/Gujarat border and less than 250 kilometres away.

Next morning, when I tell my host about my altered plans, he swiftly loses his aloofness and becomes positively hospitable. We share our final moments drinking the tea he has made.

I load my saddle-bags on to the bike and after assuring myself that everything is firmly held together by fastener straps, shake hands with Dinesh who then reflexively gives me a smart salute.

'Best of luck, Sir.'

The smooth road takes me through 150 kilometres of flat terrain before beginning a gradual climb through a forest. The motorcycle purrs all the way up.

At 1,200 metres, Mt. Abu is hardly a 'mountain', but in the otherwise flat, desert terrain of Rajasthan, it does seem impressively tall. It is noticeably cooler here. I ride into town feeling good about having left the heat of the plains behind.

This is the road that brings the town its hordes

of tourists and there are shops all around to cater to these visitors; selling the kind of things which, once back home, one is surprised to have actually paid money for. Fake ivory elephant mothers with the regulation baby elephants playing with their trunks, gods and goddesses made of red clay, *mojdis* of camel hide braided with whorls of red and green thread. There is also a profusion of bars which cater to those who come to Mt. Abu to drink the alcohol they cannot legally obtain in neighbouring 'dry' Gujarat.

I've arrived on a Saturday and many of the lodges and hotels are full but finally, I find accommodation in a boarding house located a distance away from the crowded area. 'Sri Krishna Lodge' is a row of ten rooms which stand like a train on a platform. The young T-shirt-and-blue-jeans-clad boy who is to show me the room, tells me the lodge has no kitchen of its own but with so many eateries nearby, he can bring me whatever I need. He unlocks a room in the middle of the row and bids me enter. It is a small room, occupied almost entirely by a double bed. Except for the plastic pitcher of water and a glass which are placed on the windowsill, there is nothing else. I inspect the tiny toilet and find it clean. The boy leaves me after repeating that he can get me anything I want. *'Jo chahiye woh milega'*, (You can get whatever you want), he says in a tone which covers a wide gamut of possibilities. I nod understandingly. After he's gone, I walk to my bike and begin to unload the saddle-bags.

I have just about finished when what was until a moment ago a bright and sunny sky turned suddenly dark. It took only two more minutes for lightning and thunder to pitch in with light and sound effects, and then the cloudburst descended on Mt. Abu in a torrent of welcome rain falling thick as sheets of glass.

I wait for the cloudburst to exhaust itself and when it does, it is still early evening, so I don my shoes and go out. Many people seem to have the same idea and the street is crowded. Stepping over puddles of dark brown sandy water, I walk in the direction everyone seems to be going. The road leads me to Nakki lake.

This is a picnic spot with a broad open space for the *bhelpuriwalas* and the balloon sellers. Groups of youngsters sit and stroll around the area. The lake appears to be the gathering ground for everyone, from mothers perambulating babies to members of the geriatric group.

From the *channawala,* I find out that the famous Dilwara temples are less than three kilometres away, but it is getting dark and I resolve to visit the temples tomorrow morning on my way out.

A quick dinner of *poori-bhaji* at a Rajasthani *dhaba* and it's back to my room. I clean the motorcycle and cover it with its plastic raincoat. A bath and smoke later, I slip into sleep feeling content with the way the day has gone.

I wake up early next morning. It is still dark. I feel rested and anxious to see the Dilwara temples but learn from the guesthouse office keeper that the temple complex opens for visitors only at noon.

I'm too excited to fritter away six hours of precious daylight time. The riding fever is on and it propels me to move. I'll see the Dilwara temples some other day. I intend to reach Jaipur tonight and that is 500 kilometres away. For me, it's going to be a marathon ride, the longest distance I have ever attempted in a single day. I descend Mt. Abu at 6:30 a.m., bathing in the early morning sunlight. I am on NH-14 which will keep me off the traffic-infested NH-8 until I join it again at Ajmer. I consider taking the longer road to New Delhi via Jodhpur, but that would add 350 kilometres to the trip and I drop that idea. I also consider spending the night in Pushkar which is only 17 kilometres off Ajmer. But I don't. I've been to Pushkar on a cross-country motorcycle trip Meena and I took some years ago.

Diary Entry:
Scout's Honour

It's early afternoon still and Pushkar is only nine kilometres away. The air is alive with the piercing shrieks of peacocks and the much softer chirpings of smaller birds, which abound in these forested hills. Focused on the road as I am, I don't see the scout's camp on my right. Meena, sitting pillion, points it out and I slow down, then make a U-turn to stop the Enfield next to a black metal gate with a large blue and red signboard which announces: 'Scouts Camp'.

Around five acres of the wooded terrain have been neatly fenced with steel and aluminium. It is the peacocks that first hold our attention. There are over 500 of these large birds walking about between brown canvas tents that stand abreast in neat rows of five. A few ofthe beautiful birds are dancing with their plumage fanned open. A scraggly dog with black Rorschach spots on his white coat barks from his perch on a raised stone porch outside a cemented room. The door opens and an old man, prematurely awakened from his afternoon siesta, his hands firming up the new knot of his once-white dhoti, walks towards us as we sit on the motorcycle across the closed gate. I presume he is the caretaker.

'Verma Sahab aye kya?' (Has Mr. Verma arrived?) I ask him as he approaches the gate. Meena looks at me in confusion. She doesn't know who this Mr. Verma is. She couldn't. I've just invented him. I signal her to continue keeping quiet. The man's body language tells me he has become defensive. He

salutes me, then apologetically explains that actually it is his son who is the real watchman but who had to go back to the gaon because his mother was sick and would be back only after two days. It is an age-old 'excuse' and I've heard it many times before. Have used it myself, although I'd always juggled the script a bit to replace 'sick mother' with 'dying grandfather', both my grandfathers having passed away decades ago. I let a slight understanding smile hover around my lips. I also make it a forgiving smile. But he doesn't know who we are. He's never heard of Mr. Verma either. I ask him if everything is going okay. 'Sab kuch theek hain na?'

That gets him talking. He tells us that a group of high-school students from Jaipur is expected in four days and everything has been set to accommodate them.

With a flabbergasted Meena in tow, I make a quick inspection tour of the tents, bending down to check how securely the pegs stood grounded in the rocky soil.

'Sab kuch achha hai,' ('Everything looks okay'), I pronounce my satisfaction. I ask him his name. 'Shivdayal, Sahab', he says, looking relieved. I say his son does good work; when he's around that is! I then tell him we will stay the night at the camp. 'Jee Sahab,' is now his conditioned response to anything

I say and he shows us a large single room, set a distance behind the tents. The room has ten doors and 20 windows and is probably used as a lecture hall. The lack of beds does not bother us. We have our sleeping bags. It is only 4 p.m., so we decide to make a quick trip to Pushkar and return with dinner. We must compensate him somehow for the con job we're pulling over his innocence.

So we rode to Pushkar, famous for its temple of Brahma – the only one in the world standing in a lake around which bustles Pushkar town. There was still a month to go before the annual Pushkar mela the animal fair, a major tourist draw. We walked the one main street running around the lake peeping into shops, many of which were stocked with camel leather jooties, adorned with threads of red and gold, yellow and silver. From an adjacent dhaba we got a basket full of dinner. Pooris and aloo-bhaji, also half a kilogram of hot jilebees. 'Grrrummmmm' my stomach growled in anticipation, but we would eat with Shivdayal at the campsite.

As we crested the last hill on our way back to our home for the night, we could see that the camp was located in a valley surrounded by dense forests. The full moon rose from behind the hills. It was the night of Ashwin Poornima.

It was getting chilly and Shivdayal found some

wood for a small fire. We sat around it and Meena unwrapped our dinner. Shivdayal brought out three steel plates. The jungle around us was lit up by the huge lamp in the sky. The area was abuzz with the sound of crickets. The three of us became occupied with eating our food. Shivdayal wrapped a portion of his poori around a potato and muttering a prayer, flung it towards the jungle. The harsh cry of a peacock rent the cooling air. Had he hit a sleeping bird in the eye?

Shivdayal told us his family was in the purana kapda (old clothes) business in Alwar. They scoured the bigger towns and cities exchanging old clothes for steel utensils. These clothes were reconditioned and made usable and then sold in the various village fairs around Rajasthan and Gujarat. His son had passed his high school examination. He said his son had done his family proud by landing this job with the Scouts.

I told him I wanted to take pictures of the peacocks in the morning and he assured me there would be plenty of them. He advised me not to make any noise or sudden movements as I approached them with my camera, as they were notoriously shy birds, jumping away at the slightest hint of threat. I thanked him and he thanked me. He walked to his hut and we went into our bedroom which had many wide-open windows for the moonlight to seep in and bathe us in silver.

Hyenas howled for mates all through that night but I had mine and didn't need to.

It was at 6 o'clock in the morning that the timid knocking on one of the doors woke us. Must be the old man come with tea? I remembered I had to get my peacock pictures. I opened the door to see a thin, small-statured woman in brown scout's shorts and blue scarf, red beret in hand standing with two others who looked like students and were also in uniform.

'Excuse me Sir.'

'You're excused,' I said to put her at ease but she didn't see the humour and good scout that she was, decided to obey my order. She tried her best to look excused!

'We are scouts from xyz Company, abc Division travelling from Ahmedabad. Thirty children Sir, in the bus. Can we rest here for three hours Sir? The children are quite tired Sir, after a night's travel Sir.' It dawned on me that these were real scouts who had every right to use this camp. And here they were almost begging me, an impostor, for permission which I had no real authority to give or withhold. So of course I gave it but with a clause or two of my own. I warned them not to make any noise. It

would disturb the peacocks. The lady promised me the children would be very quiet indeed and was also quite profuse in her expressions of gratitude for what she saw as my magnanimity. After some more 'Thank you, Sirs,' she backed away in the manner of courtiers not turning their backs on their monarch.

In the end it was an unrealistic assurance that she gave me. To expect thirty children to all stay quiet for three hour. The peacocks knew better and didn't come to the camp ground that morning. Not one. I should have taken the pictures last evening.

By 9 a.m., we ourselves were ready to leave for Jaipur. As we wished Shivdayal goodbye, he promised me he would inform Mr. Verma I had inspected the camp and had pronounced it all right. But could I please write a small note confirming my satisfaction? I didn't see any reason why I couldn't do that and wrote down my report, generously studding it with superlatives, even suggesting that the old man's son be given a raise. Why not? My recommendations might even be taken seriously. This was India where strange things happen all the time. The written word somehow carries great weight in this country run by over-worked bureaucrats. I added an SN after my name, not knowing myself what official position it implied. Samanya Nagrik (common citizen) perhaps?

I also assured him I wouldn't tell anyone about his son playing the absentee game. He gave Meena a peacock feather as a parting gift. Both impostors of a kind, Shivdayal and I parted with a quiet respect for each other.

Viva la zindagee!

But no Pushkar this time.

Today I've got Ladakh on my mind.

These old tar roads winding through the blazing desert sands, are not heavily trafficked and that makes them a biker's delight. It's cactus and sand country. Brown and more brown all around me. About noon it is toasting hot – must be 50°C. Roadside teashops quench my thirst with cups of superb tea.

Sufi Baba

At one such tea stall, my digital camera is a big attraction. The half a dozen bare-chested truck drivers and the owner of the *dhaba* love to see their own pictures instantly. I sit on the *charpai* and share tales. As I am having my last cup of *chai*, I see an old man, dressed in a long green gown, cycling away on the sun-soaked road in the direction I was going. I say my goodbyes to the truckers as I finish my tea, then mount my steed and on the road again. I soon overtake the old man's cycle, ride on a bit ahead to a culvert where I stop and wait for him to arrive.

At first glance, it would be easy to mistake him for a bone-thin, weak old man. But as he gets closer, it is apparent that his wiry limbs appear thin only because there is no fat on them. His hard-muscled legs pedal the cycle. but in the hazy glare of the sun reflecting off the shiny road, he himself seems to be floating towards me with the ends of his long white beard fluttering in the slight breeze. His head protected by a white turban tied with a bright blue scarf, a black and white chequered cotton shawl around his shoulders, he slows down when he sees me waiting for him at the culvert.

'*Salaam Waleykum*,' I greet him and he acknowledges with a slight nod. After some initial hesitation, he alights and puts his cycle up on its stand. His bicycle, an older model of the most common design, with its traditional handlebar curved at each end and its old-fashioned rear carrier, says several things about its owner. Spotlessly clean and well lubricated, it has space for a jerry can of water and on the large rear carrier is a rolled bedding and an old canvas bag. A hammock made of gunnysack is ingeniously suspended below the front bar and this is how he must carry his food without it being squashed. A rear view mirror and an Indian flag share space on the front handle with a largish notice written on a tin plate, which has information about his trip.

Silently he sits next to me on the culvert with only the sound of an occasional truck roaring past to punctuate the silence.

No words pass between us for many minutes. There appears no need for them. His eyes look far away into the horizon and their gaze is benevolent. He sits motionless for about five minutes.

When he finally moves, it was to bring out a packet

of *bidis,* seeing which I am emboldened to bring out my own cigarette pack and light up for both of us. He talks then. Asks me my whereabouts. I ask him his.

He said he is cycling from Vasai (near Mumbai) to Ajmer and then on to Mecca.

'Mecca? But that's in Saudi Arabia!' I exclaim as if he didn't know that. I realize I am mirroring the amazed reactions my own journey had elicited only two days ago from my sister in Dahanu, when I told her how far Ladakh was. I wonder what she would have had to say to this bearded old *fakir*.

'Baba, *Kuchh kahiye*' (say something), which is what my mother would say to anyone in whom she sensed a degree of spiritual power. The cinder-dark face with its halo of white hair beams at me with eyes sparkling, but the man stays quiet.

My voice is tinged with the doubts I couldn't help feeling when I ask, 'How long will it take for you to reach Mecca?'

He looks skywards and says he is there already.

'Sirf badan ko wahan le jaana hai.
Rooh to wahin rahtee hai.'

He was merely transporting his body to where his soul already lived. This journey was just a matter of satisfying a detail and whether or not he actually succeeds in getting to Mecca really did not matter. It would be Mecca for him wherever his body breathed its last breath. That day he is planning to cover 100 kilometres at 15 kilometres per hour all the way to Pali.

'*Kahaan rahenge*?' (Where will you stay?) I ask.

'*Khuda ki is shahi duniya mein, sone ke liye, do gaz zameen to mil hi jaati hai.*'

(On God's palatial earth, one can always find two yards of space to sleep.)

He refuses to take money from me and only after some Hindi filmi sounding dialogues '*Babaji, kuchh mera nahi hai… Aatee jaatee maya hai*', ('Nothing is really mine… Just a passing illusion'), does he accept a small portion of what I give him. When I ask why he had returned most of the money, he gently inquires if I had time to listen to a story.

Sitting on the culvert, I nod my head.

'This is the story of a young monk who had lived a cloistered life in a remote monastery where all other initiates were males like him,' begins the old man as he puffs on his *bidi*.

I pull my legs up to sit cross-legged on the parapet and feel like a young child being told a story by his grandfather. The old man smiles and continues:

On his eighteenth birthday, his master sends the boy out into the world to spread the teachings of their Grand Master amongst the common people. He was to survive by begging for his meals in the time-honoured *bhikshuk* tradition.

Descending from the mountain monastery. which was the only abode the young man has known in his life thus far, the sights and sounds of the city streets amaze him. Odd creatures walk around, mixing with the men of the city. Male children he has seen before but these other creatures who look strange, dress, walk and speak differently, are a mystery to him.

Soon he is hungry. As he has been instructed, he holds his begging bowl in his hands and stands near the threshold of a small dwelling. The householder welcomes the young monk in and washes his feet to show respect. He then calls his teenaged daughter who walks into the room and fills the monk's bowl with grain; enough for that day and the next seven. She joins her hands in a graceful *namaste* and smiles a respectful greeting.

The young man cannot now hold back his questions. He asks the man who the creature is and is told. He points to her breasts and asks what they are. The father of the girl knows about the all-male cloisters of monks who live in the higher regions in absolute seclusion until they become eighteen years old. He is not offended by the innocent questions. He explains the purpose of breasts. In some years, his daughter would be married and milk from her breasts would feed the babies she would bear.

The young man stands still in contemplation for a while and then hastily returns all the extra grain that he has taken. He says he will accept food enough for that one day only. And when the householder asks him why he was returning a major portion of the offering, the initiate turns to him and answers: 'My master told me to take enough only for one day. I disobeyed him when I took more than what I would need for today. But I now see my mistake in being concerned about tomorrow. When arrangements are already in place to provide food for a child who will be born many days from today, I am a fool to worry about what I will eat tomorrow.'

Baba finishes his story and his second *bidi* and gets up. Before continuing on his journey, the venerable man raises both arms heavenwards and says a prayer for my safety.

He pulls up his lungi and gets up on his cycle by swinging his leg over the front bar. With his gaze on the road ahead, he begins to pedal away. I watch him fade into the afternoon heat.

A genuine Sufi king, travelling incognito.

Oh… Wondrous India!

Yak Ghee for a Yagna

Not all *sadhus* I met were saints. Later on, that same day, I feel the brakes need some tightening and stop under the shade of a sprawling banyan tree, squat to take out my tool kit and locate the spanner I need. It is only a minor readjustment and does not take much time. Repacking my tools, I look up to see two *sadhus*, complete with ash and iron chains staring down at me. With clean white *lungis* knotted at the navel and saffron shawls over their bare shoulders, they look dressed for the role.

I can feel their eyes quickly assess my worth. No one who has lived in India for any length of time has escaped such encounters and after a while one becomes adept in sifting the genuine *sadhu* from the husk of impostors. These two are at the business end of wearing saffron.

Needing a break from the ride anyway, I decide to play their game and have some fun too, energized as I feel from my recent encounter with the powerful Sufi *fakir*. I pretend supplication and bend down to touch their feet. As I raise myself, my eyes catch the fag end of the knowing smile the older con exchanges with his *chela*. To them I must look like a good prospective *bakra* and without delay they launch their efforts to relieve me of some of my earthly wealth.

But there is nothing innovative about their particular approach. It is an age-old modus operandi. Not much different from what hospitals and insurance or security agencies do to drum up clientele. Scare them by telling them what all can go wrong. Warn sternly that disasters can happen to them, and then, once they are adequately afraid, assure them that assuaging the gods through their own good offices could prevent the occurrence of all bad future events. Scare-Warn-Reassure. These two ash-covered men work their craft along these same lines. I decide to indulge them for a while longer and continue to act stupid, nodding my head as the older one talks about some of their numerous successes at healing the sick or enriching the poor. I pretend to look impressed and I am sure they think they have me in their net. I wait for their hook to land. In the end, even I am flattered by their estimate of my worth. A thousand rupees would do the trick with their *devi mata*, says the older one.

I let out a loud guffaw. which takes them completely by surprise. The older one understands that I've been playing my own game with them. For the first time, his eyes lose their avarice and take on a pleading look. The small amount of money I give them anyway falls well short of their expectations and they desperately start to hound me for more. Enough at least, for one kilogram of pure *ghee*, which they promise to use in a *yagna* to generate good luck for me on the trip. Exasperated, I tell them I'll bring them the finest yak *ghee* from Ladakh and kick-start the engine.

It is time to move on.

Once I rejoin NH-8, the ride from Ajmer to Jaipur becomes a test of endurance. With much of the new highway, part of the 'golden quadrilateral', still under construction, diversions are the order of the day. Traffic is heavy. NH-8 is the lifeline of the country and brimming with laden trucks carrying everything from steel and stone to finished industrial goods. By 6 p.m. the sand begins to blow across the road and in spite of the visor, its grains find access to my nose and eyes. I've been riding for ten hours since I'd left Mt. Abu. As the golden evening begins to turn into twilight, I start to look for a lodge.

After 7 o'clock it becomes dark, which dramatically decreases odds of survival. With high-beam halogen lights from trucks coming the other way blinding me, the dark visor is now a hindrance and has to be drawn up to improve visibility and prevent the motorcycle from hitting any of the many potholes or in some places, large rocks left lying on the road. The sand is still blowing and hits my eyeballs with disturbing impact. This, I tell myself, was what I got from breaking my own rule of not riding after sunset. Now I am caught on the dark highway with not an exit in sight. The unmade road seems to go on and on with nowhere to stop. Truck after laden truck, at times crawling bumper to bumper. Sometimes without warning, a driver breaks out of the orderly convoy in a burst of impatient speed. I could have died ten times but ten times I didn't. I become one up on cats. The old Sufi's blessings are doing their job!

It is close to 10 p.m. when I settle for a seedy highway lodge where a large but un-ventilated room beckons me uninvitingly to a lonely bed. These last hot hours on the highway to Jaipur have painted me black in skin and spirit. A quick shower in a candlelit bathroom and an unremembered dinner later, slumber land opens its gates and lets me enter. My last thought that day is 'Phew… what a ride!'

But I did not know what was in store.

The Manali-Leh road was waiting.

Jaipur 6 a.m. Clean the grime and dust off the bike. Top up the engine oil. Two cups of tea and an omelette-*paratha* breakfast later, I am on the four-lane Jaipur-Delhi highway with 250 kilometres of high speed riding ahead and the sun blazing overhead.

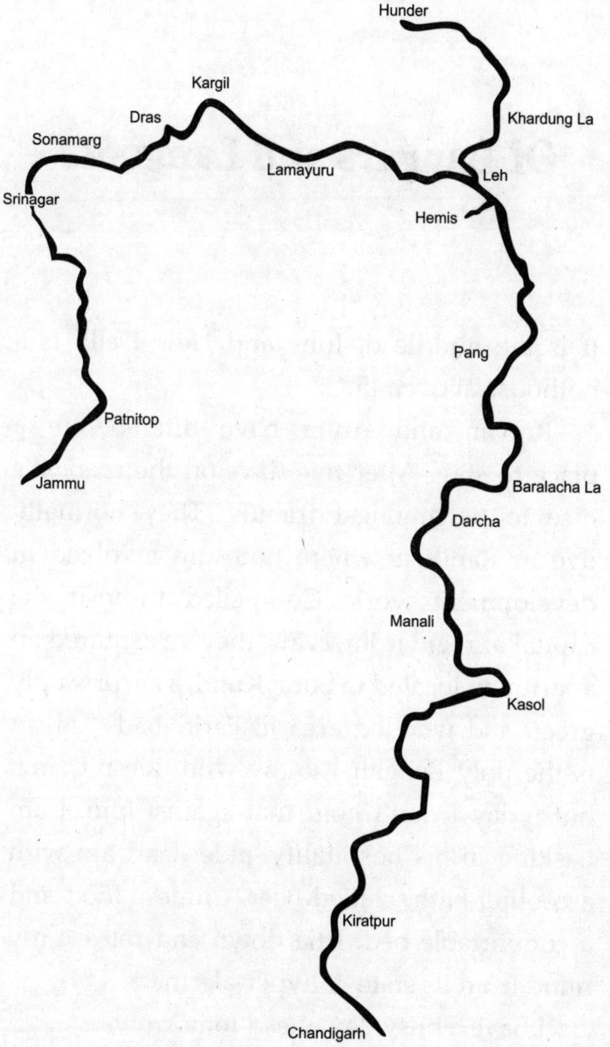

Route Map from Chandigarh to the high Himalayas.

Of Langars and Langoors

It is the middle of June and New Delhi is a hothouse at over 45°C.

Kalyan and Anita have offered me a place to stay. After five days on the road, it's nice to be amongst friends. They normally live in Ranikhet where both are involved in development work. Compelled to visit the capital at regular intervals, they've acquired an apartment located in Suraj Kund, a surprisingly green and wooded area in Faridabad. Kalyan is the only Bengali I know who doesn't sing, but today I don't hold that against him. I am basking in his hospitality, aided as I am with a cooling bath, chilled beer, Chinese food and a comfortable bed. I lie down and release my mind from its state of hyper-alertness.

I have a busy day ahead tomorrow.

Riding the Enfield through 10 a.m. week day Delhi traffic is a skill that demands complete concentration. I am headed towards Karol Bagh which is a Mecca for the Enfield enthusiast with entire shops devoted to this particular brand of motorcycle. I have to get mine fitted with side luggage carriers to hold the two canisters of fuel I would need later on in the ride. I walk into a shop that has what I want. I also get a broad rubber foot grip for the brake pedal and webbing nets to hold the luggage more firmly. And three litres of engine oil – the lifeblood of my bike.

It takes two hours to get the new carriers fixed. The heat is draining me. There are five days to go before my web group meets in Delhi, and the thought of bearing this climate is not at all appealing. I must leave Delhi and head for the hills.

Kalyan has told me about a college friend of his who runs a chalet-hotel in Kasol, near Manali and from the picture he has painted of deodar forests, mountain rivers and lovely weather, Kasol is where I decide to go.

I sms the group that I am leaving Delhi and will meet them in Manali.

There are two routes to Manali. One goes via Shimla and Narkhanda, over the Jalori Pass which the Internet grapevine says is steep and could prove difficult. I take the easier option and settle on the route that goes via Chandigarh and Kiratpur.

The next morning, just as it is time to leave, the skies become unexpectedly suffused with dark clouds and soon open up with a welcome shower of heavy rain. For a while, the way it is pouring, I consider delaying my departure by another day; but by 10 a.m., the sky has cleared and I decide to get on the road. The north-bound highway is modern and makes the ride to Chandigarh fast and uneventful.

Past the Chandigarh bypass, I begin to get a feel of the prosperous and aggressively generous ambience of rural Punjab. The state highways are smooth and free of potholes but not wide enough for the light and heavy vehicles that are zipping past each other with not much room to spare between them. Not the kind of riding a biker enjoys. The sight of three fresh accidents (one of them fatal) does nothing to make me alter my defensive-minded riding. Maintaining such mental alertness all day long can get fatiguing and by the time I approach the foothills of the Himalayas, I am anxiously looking for a place to stay for the night.

Hotels along the road, few as they are, have a gaudy plastic ambience to them with rates I don't feel like paying. So I keep on riding. At a *chai* shop, the Sikh owner interrupts the brushing of his long hair, his cupped palm holding hair oil, to tell me about the *gurudwara* at Kiratpur where I could stay the night for free. Two more hours of riding this busy highway demands total attention.

Around 6 o'clock in the evening, I come upon the white *gurudwara* located across a small gushing river. Just as I ride over the metal bridge, a swarm of crag-martins whooshes over my head.

The setting sun has bathed the white marble dome of the *gurudwara* in a hue of glittering gold. I can hear the *shabad* being sung inside. I switch off the engine but sit astride the bike and listen.

Two male voices are singing to the accompaniment of a harmonium and *tabla*. I can feel the compassion in their resonant voices.

I park the bike and walk towards a room which has 'OFFICE' painted over its door. A white-turbaned middle-aged Sikh sitting behind a small wooden desk, is friendly and says yes, a room could be provided. He tells me to sign my name in the register, then looking at it, asks if I was a Sikh; not that that made a difference, he assures without waiting for my answer. The *gurudwara* is open to everyone and everything including the room and the food is completely free.

'As it should be in any house of God,' he says in Punjabi.

I ask him what the *shabad* singers are saying. He repeats the verse I've just heard and tells me what it means.

"Kaheyrey ban khojan jayee
Sarva nivasi sada alefa
Tuhi sang samahee."

(Why are you looking for the divine all over the jungles? The all existent One also exists within you.)

I am issued two mattresses, a pillow and a white sheet. A clean-shaven man in his thirties shows me my room. He suggests that I park the motorcycle with me in the room. I first think he is joking but he doesn't look like he is. I tell him I had thought that a *gurudwara* would be a safe enough place and he assures me it still is. His accompanying smile only deepens my doubt but he does not say anything further on the matter. Instead, informs me I can eat at the evening *langar* which is open from 7 to 8 o'clock. Every *gurudwara* anywhere in the world offers free meals to anyone who wants them.

The room I'm shown is just that – a room with a door and a single window opening on to the corridor. In contrast to the rest of the *gurudwara* complex, the bathroom is surprisingly shabby, almost filthy. But the tap provides a strong gush of sparkling clean water, which hits the sore muscles of my back with therapeutic force.

I know it is against the rules but I think I've earned it and gulp down a swallow of the rum I've been carrying in a hip flask. I then spend five minutes brushing my teeth and cleansing my mouth of any telltale hints of alcohol. Time for dinner. I walk towards the *langar* building which is set aside from the main *gurudwara*.

I climb up broad marbled steps and enter the dining hall but am stopped at the door by a Sikh youth who points to my head. I have forgotten to cover my head. I have left my own grease-soiled handkerchief in the room. The young man hands me a piece of square cloth taken off a bunch hanging from a nail on the wall for exactly such a contingency.

The *langar* is on. Over 50 men, women and children of all ages sit in rows on the stone floor and are in various stages of completing their meals. I find myself seated between two elderly men in tattered clothes. Across us sit two men who look like rich businessmen. No distinction of creed or status influences the servers of the hot *rotis*and the *dal*. The *rotis* have to be accepted with folded hands, whoever the hands belong to. At the Guru's *langar*, we are all beggars. Basic *dal-roti* though it was, the food replenishes both spiritual and bodily nutrients.

Dinner done, I walk back to the room allotted to me, still not sure why I have been asked to park my motorcycle next to my bed. I do it anyway, roll the machine over the slight protuberance of the threshold and thumpkk... into the room it is. The actual reason for this baffling action becomes apparent only around 9 p.m., when ten busloads of Sikh families descend on the *gurudwara* and soon every inch of the corridor is covered with rolled out mattresses and clusters of luggage.

From inside my room, I can hear their excited talk. Punjabi is not too difficult to understand if you know Hindi and I eavesdrop on snatches of dialogue.

A gruff male voice is telling someone about the bank instalments he has to pay for his tractor.

A mother is cooing to her bawling infant.

Gradually everyone has settled down and now it is suddenly very quiet but for a pair of snorers who croon everyone a lullaby in and out of synchrony.

Kiratpur is in a valley and the road begins to ascend in a steep incline almost immediately as I ride out of the ornate canopy-like gate of the *gurudwara* the next morning. After only a few minutes of this road, the engine begins to stutter. It is being starved of air. Flat land is at a premium but I find a bit of it and park the bike to adjust the carburettor to a newer setting for air intake. This barely takes five minutes and the engine regains a passably healthy beat. I plan to get the bike serviced at Manali before I get on to the road to Leh. Being preoccupied with matters mechanical, I haven't realized that all this while, I've had an audience of over 50 small and big *langoors* who have been watching me with avid interest. Now, as I look at them, some begin to make faces, while others sprint around for a better view of me, their evolutionary goal. I switch off the engine and look around. It is a panoramic setting; rolling green hills interspaced with ploughed brown farmland and with the snow-laden higher mountains, white in the backdrop. The soft cool breeze – gentle now but soon to gain strength as I make my way higher.

Then it begins to rain and the road becomes messy. I detour through a longish tunnel and come to a turn towards Kasol – 30 kilometres off the road to Manali. A gentle drizzle grows into some serious rain. I stop for *chai* at a roadside *dhaba*. The two-roomed tin shack is being managed by two young locals who are around 20 years old. They are friendly and we exchange comments about the weather and the road. As one begins to make the tea I have asked for, the other lights up a cigarette which soon betrays its contents by the sweet acrid aroma that spreads across the tiny room. After a deep pull on the joint, he offers it to me.

'*Abhi nahein*,' (not now) I say but maybe my refusal is too abrupt and there is a sudden wary look in his eyes.

'*Aap army mein hain*?'(Are you from the army?) he asks and appears noticeably reassured when I tell him I'm neither army nor police. Right now, I am concerned only about reaching Kasol without mishap. That was the kind of narrow, twisting, potholed, frequently slushy road it was, all 22 kilometres of it.

The rain has fizzled into a drizzle as I enter Kasol which is a village with shops and hotels on either side of the main road, all geared up for tourists. My destination, Alpine Crest Hotel is two buildings standing on the banks of a gushing river. The roar of the water masks all other sounds, even the beat of the Enfield; and Sanjoy, Kalyan's friend and owner of the hotel, hasn't heard me arrive. Kalyan has shown me a picture of them together in which both were dressed in suit and tie. That was taken on graduation day. Today Sanjoy is dressed in faded jeans and a black T-shirt which has seen many winters.

He is supervising the construction of a new roof for his house. I yell out a loud 'Hi' and he comes over to where I'm standing and says he's been expecting me.

I have been allotted a room on the ground floor facing the river. 'River Parvati' (Sanjoy fills in the name), rushing down from the mountains. Glittering. Playful. Powerful. Studded with boulders which must have a lot of mica in them – they sparkle like mirrors. The roar of the river doesn't make for easy conversation. And it seems almost blasphemous to talk loudly in its presence. What can we say that the ancient river hasn't heard before?

I look around the wooded estate. Pine and deodar trees tower all around me. Bright red begonias in pots line the balconies of the hotel while vines of vibrant yellow flowers creep contrastingly over the rough stone walls. The fragrance of deodar is in the chill evening air. Sanjoy is busy – his sister is arriving with her family the next day and he has to get some things in order.

I have an early dinner and snuggle into bed. Two days ago in Delhi, even a thin cotton sheet over my body had been intolerable. Today I'm shivering pleasurably under the thickly quilted *razai*. I hug the clean white pillow and fall asleep. The sound of the rapidly flowing waters forms a canvas for my dreams. I dream of flying over oceans and plunging down waterfalls.

I also make frequent trips to the toilet.

The next day's ride takes me to Manikaran, only four kilometres away, where hot springs and the massive *gurudwara* are the places to visit. The narrow bridge connecting the *gurudwara* to the road hung over my dream mate, the river Parvati. Manikaran is also a destination point for trekkers and I pass two groups who are walking upwards, everyone carrying a hefty backpack.

I return to my room. It is June 22, my last evening in Kasol. I get busy servicing the bike and packing the saddle-bags. Dinner. Sleep. Then it is morning and time to get on the road.

'Tranquil' is the word to describe the road to Manali. I feel rested and refreshed. The river has soothed me. I've avoided the busy Kulu-Manali highway and have taken the much less frequented Naggar road which meanders through forests of deodars. These huge trees with life spans of two or even three centuries watch over me with seeming munificence. The sun filters in through the dense foliage of the treetops.

I slow down to let a large, plump mongoose mother with two young ones cross the road but the sound of the approaching motorcycle has scared her and halfway across, she loses nerve and turns around to rush back to where she started from.

Fortified by an omelette, *paratha* and two cups of tea I have at a *dhaba*, I enter Manali (2,050 metres).

This resort town could very well be renamed 'Hotel Alley'. Every standing structure is a hotel. The narrow streets of Manali wind around at steep angles and finding a flat patch of land to park my bike becomes the criterion on which I choose the small single-storeyed, stone-roofed hotel which overlooks the river Beas.

Across the milky white frothing river is a fenced-in forest of thousands of closely packed deodars. My hotel room is small and clean and quite affordable at Rs. 150 per day. As good a place as any for the two days I plan to spend in Manali. That is the period I've been advised to stay here to acclimatize the body to the rarer high altitude atmosphere.

I spend the next day strolling around town, buying up provisions – mainly chocolates, biscuits and five litres of bottled water. Drink lots of fluids – the experts on the web have cautioned me. Don't smoke or drink alcohol, they've added. High Altitude Pulmonary Edema (HAPE) can affect anyone regardless of age or level of physical fitness. It is known to strike at altitudes above 3,000 metres. Symptoms can include severe shortness of breath, hacking cough and fever. I've got a strip of the recommended Diamox 250 mg tablets and swallow one before dinner.

I have been in sporadic contact with the group I was supposed to be travelling with. Now Subash, the person I've talked to but not seen, sends an sms to tell me that they are approaching Manali and I guide them to my hotel, then go and book rooms for them.

My four co-riders-to-be arrive late that evening, looking impressively dust-covered. After half a month of riding alone, I had company at last. As they take off their helmets, I see all of them are around 25 years old. I had read their introductions on the Yahoo group site and knew that Subash and Mani both worked for Infosys in Bangalore and had flown to Delhi, then rented a 500 cc Enfield which they rode between themselves.

In his light brown leather jacket, and with his mop of curly hair crowning a pleasant debonair face, Subash cuts an attractive figure. 'Ditcher!' is the first word he greets me with and the way the other three are looking at me, I can see they all agreed that I was guilty of a serious misdemeanour when I left Delhi without the group. It takes some explaining but gradually they thaw and soon the vibes between us become positive and pleasant. Mani, Subash's riding buddy is a quiet, introspective kind of guy who does not say much but had an easy body language.

Varun is a six-footer from Ahmedabad who spends most of his time talking to his new wife on his mobile. He is the only son of an industrialist and at first glance looks an unlikely figure to be attempting such an arduous journey. One could more easily associate him with 'couch-potato' activities but appearances can be deceptive because he has ridden his Enfield all the way from Ahmedabad.

Prem, the fourth member of the group has come to Delhi from Mumbai with his bike on the train. He is an expert motorcycle mechanic, very knowledgeable about the Enfield, easily falling into intense emotional debate over the desirability of gas-filled shock absorbers or how important it was to coat the inside of the petrol tank with a layer of Teflon ('to prevent internal rust').

My first evening with my friends is also my last in Manali. We share a bottle of Old Monk and sing a few Hindi songs. For dinner we walk over to a nearby open air restaurant and by the time we return to the hotel it is already 11 p.m.

I like to begin the day's ride early and all these days, I have been in saddle at the break of dawn. But it looks like my young friends are all late risers and it is 10 a.m. by the time we are all ready to take off.

Only 25 kilometres out of Manali, my bike begins to lose power and within minutes, the engine has developed a staccato beat. It is also getting overly heated. The Manali-Leh stretch has just begun and I am already in serious trouble. I stop to let the engine cool. I have been riding ahead of the gang who have probably stopped somewhere behind. I start the bike after a ten-minute wait but can go only half a kilometre before the engine begins to protest, this time with much greater vehemence. Stop. Wait. Think. The engine is radiating even more intense heat and that is a very bad sign indeed. At this temperature, the piston could well be on the verge of choking. I can't risk going ahead now. I will have to roll the bike down to Manali and get the problem fixed. That will mean a delay of one day if not more, and I will miss attending the Hemis festival which is one of the high points of the trip. Damn! I sit on a nearby stone and ruminate on my misfortune. I look up and send out a plea for help. And as we all know, God is great. Ten minutes is all it takes for Him to make His emissary appear.

He comes in the form of Prem who parks his bike alongside mine and after I've told him what happened, asks if I have my tools with me. Twenty minutes later, Prem has got the engine back to a healthy beat. I ask him what the matter was and he goes into a lengthy explanation using words like 'tappets', 'rods', 'cam shafts', etc. I can't say I understand half of it. But I am saved. That's all I am thinking about. I say my thanks to Prem. And thanks to the group. All thoughts of the disadvantages of our late departure have disappeared. But now my faith in the infallibility of my bike has been shaken. The road ahead is 475 kilometres of one of the roughest and most desolate terrains on earth.

The altitude is another factor I cannot ignore. Although I have not felt any of the symptoms that could signal the onset of high altitude sickness, I have read that they can appear quite suddenly and are capable of inducing incapacitating headaches and intense nausea. Who would help me then? The presence of the group is reassuring. Subash suggests I ride ahead. If I have further trouble with the bike, they would be riding behind me and could help me out again. We plan to camp together in Darcha, which we expect to reach before dark.

As I take off, my last view of the group is of Mani taking video pictures of a pair of white vultures who are necking (or are they quarrelling?) on an extended branch of a tree that jutts out from the sides of the valley below the climbing road. The road from Manali to Rohtang La is nicely paved and it is an easy ascent to Rohtang La (3,980 metres). This historic pass between Kullu and Lahaul valleys offers the first spectacular view of the higher Himalayas and is a popular northernmost stop on the tourist itinerary.

The atmosphere at the top of Rohtang is carnival. Noise from tape recorders mingles with fumes from a hundred diesel vehicles, the smell of *chhole-parathe* from the *dhabas*, the cries of balloon-sellers, the excited yelps of children enjoying their pony rides. But once I crest the Rohtang, the ambience changes as if by magic. Silence takes over. Not a soul in sight for long stretches.

The Journey begins with Meena doing a Pooja

Juhi wants to hop on the bike

Sufi Baba

A sadhu's blessings

Waiting for a customer, a roadside barber near Ajmer admires himself

River Parvati in Kasol

Chocolate with Vanilla topping

With Jawans of Karnataka Regiment

Baralacha La

Tanglang-La - the tough one

Hemis Festival

Dancer-Hemis Festival

FarmerTsering Motup in Hunder

Juhi on Ice- Khardung La

Maratha Regiment

Back home with Juhi

Beyond the Rohtang La

A pair of white eagles circles overhead in an aerial ballet in the absolutely blue sky. I have mentally travelled this road when reading the write-ups previous travellers had posted on the Internet. But now that I am actually riding my dream, the road speaks to me one-to-one. I didn't know roads could talk. This one does, exuding warmth and welcome. Moving away from habitation at 30 kilometres per hour with Khoksar still hours ahead, my new friend keeps me entertained through road signs to make me laugh and keep me alert. One says: 'Darling I love you, but not so fast!' Another challenges: 'On my curve, check your nerve.' Yet another advises everyone to 'Drive on horse power, not on rum power.' The BRO (Border Roads Organization) must have a wry sense of humour. They must need it too. All along the route from Manali to Leh and northwards towards Siachen, then westwards to Srinagar, the BRO maintains these high altitude roads, some of which get washed away by glacial melt every afternoon and have to be rebuilt every evening.

By early afternoon I come to Khoksar, a sparse habitation with a few shops and shelters on either side of the road. Here, on a wooden table painted green, I have my first of the '*dal*-rice' meals, which is staple food in these areas. The only other choice offered on the menu is instant noodles.

A hundred kilometres from Manali is Tandi, a significant dot on the map because here is where one tanks up on petrol. An ominous sign has warned me that there is no petrol available over the next 375 kilometres but I have been alerted to this through the grapevine and have come prepared. The gas station is a single-pump affair. The attendant is a friendly young fellow and helps me top up 14.5 litres in the tank and also fills the two extra three-litre cans I got fitted in Delhi.

River Bhaga keeps me company as I enter Keylong, just eight kilometres away from Tandi.

Keylong surprises me with its size and modernity. There are shops selling just about everything – from food, fruits, vegetables, to consumer goods like TVs and refrigerators. There are Chinese restaurants and schools with smiling children dressed in vivid uniforms. There is a BSNL tower to give good connectivity on my mobile. I compose a collective 'wish you were here' message and send it to my friends.

Keylong looks like a 'happening' place. I would have liked to stay here a while longer but Darcha, which is to be my halt for the night, is still 40 kilometres away and I want to reach it before dark.

Afternoons are a glorious time to be riding a motorcycle on narrow gravel roads which snake through the Himalayas. With the sun already close to the peaks, the play of light colours the landscape in shades that vary from bright yellow to gleaming gold. At this altitude, I'm now moving much above the tree line and there is not a patch of green to be seen anywhere. I am alone again; my group has still not caught up with me and I've been going at a speed of no more than 20 kilometres per hour. Perhaps I'll see them in Darcha.

Soon the narrow road begins to broaden and in the distance I can now see a few large circular tents next to the river Bhaga which has been flowing alongside all this while.

Darcha will never qualify if it is its 'night life' one is talking about. With just about two tent hotels and a police checkpoint (another tent), this is a desolate place.

The Himachal Pradesh state policeman asks me to go inside the police station to register my passage. When asked why, he explains that it helps them trace riders in case they are lost. Since time was all we had, he elaborates with a story of the month before, when two foreigners had been killed and their embassies had wanted such details.

After these formalities are completed, the policeman walks with me towards a large tent – the first of the two 'hotels' here, and orders tea from the Tibetan owner. As we sip the welcome hot and sweet beverage, he tells me his name is Vir Singh and he is from Mandi. Like most of the army personnel I met all along my journey, Vir Singh is also thoroughly bored of his current posting and can talk of nothing except his upcoming annual leave when he could go back to his family. We talk for a while and then I walk towards the tent to arrange for my accommodation.

The main entrance, which is really a flap of thick canvas, has been tied open and I peep into the circular tent, which looks large enough to house two cricket teams including the substitutes and umpires! I count a total of 40 metal beds (with mattresses and thick quilts on each) placed in rows of eight, separated by foot-wide aisles on either side.

The hotel is operated by a Tibetan couple whose own space is cordoned off from the guest beds by a curtain of some more thick brown canvas.

Another area has three wooden tables painted a garish green around which a few plastic chairs are placed for guests to eat their breakfast and dinner.

Not many have lunch in Darcha, except perhaps a few passing travellers and of course Vir Singh and the Tibetan couple themselves.

'Joley,' the tent keeper smiles me his greeting. Like most Tibetans, he is a man of few words. Picking up my unloaded saddle-bags, I follow him to a corner away from where he and his wife have their alcove of semi-privacy. There is no one else, so I have a choice of 40 beds.

The menu for dinner again lists the same *dal*-rice combo but I facilitate that with some Old Monk rum and am content to go to sleep before the clock strikes nine. My last thought is that my biking friends have still not made an appearance. Wonder what happened?

Getting up at two in the morning to purge myself of some liquid, I try to get out of the tent but find the strings so securely tied that they are difficult to unknot. Oh yes. It is also pitch dark inside. Tucked away in my jacket I have a tiny torch which I use to locate and finally open the flap door and rush into the freezing cold outside, just about in time to pass some pee which steams vapour as it rushes out of my over-laden bladder.

Ahhhh! Relief.

It is cold; with my hands tucked deep into the warm side pockets of my high altitude jacket, I walk towards the river, iridescent on my left like a huge silver anaconda snaking through stony banks. The sky is adorned with a rising, nearly full moon – the peaks all around highlighted against the shimmering sky.

But the cold begins to get through the thick woollen cap into my head and I have to return to the warmth of the tent within the hour.

When morning dawns, I quickly eat a noodle breakfast and kick my faithful Enfield to life. I have already said my goodbye to a sleepy Vir Singh over a last cup of tea. I also write out a message to Subash informing him about my plan to camp in Pang on that day. Vir Singh promises to give the note to the group when they passed through Darcha.

I have read on the web that the 80-kilometre ride from Darcha to Sarchu is a tough one. My main worry is to be the *nallahs* formed by glacial melt, which run across the roads like small rivers. The flow of water also washes away parts of the road which then becomes a collection of loose 'stones' offering very little purchase for tyres and often resulting in the rider losing control over his vehicle. A broken leg can be a major calamity on this isolated road.

Apprehensive as I am at the beginning of the day's ride, I would later be able to classify it as one of the most exciting of the trip.

The road is taking me through some more barren terrain before beginning to climb. The bike is doing very well since Prem worked his magic on it yesterday. The steep incline poses no problem and the engine purrs effortlessly in spite of the altitude and the load it is pulling.

Suddenly, around a narrow bend a blue lake appears on my right and I stop, put the bike up on its stand and look around. This must be Suraj Tal, a lake like no other I've seen. It fills the valley almost to the brim and its blue waters look absolutely still. No fish plops, no butterflies flutter over it. Snow-laden peaks stand reflected in it with crystal clear certainty. It's an ethereal landscape with me to experience it all alone. I sit cross-legged on a large flat black stone, a seat that is tailor-made for any aspiring guru to meditate on. Presently, without warning, the wind makes its entry and begins to blow in increasingly firm gusts. The waters are now rippling with excitement as the strong wind caresses the surface of the lake, whispering secrets which I'm not privy to.

I am filled with a sense of awe and wonder. I'm in the midst of powerful natural forces which can crush me without effort but choose not to. I can only surrender to this bliss and feel enthralled.

Ten minutes here seem too few but I cannot afford to linger longer. Daylight is precious and I remount my metal steed, reassured when the now-cooled engine starts without the help of the choke. The road continues its journey towards the sky.

Glacier melt has washed out some sections and icy water runs over some patches, but I have covered my socks with plastic bags and my feet are warm and dry as I ride around hair-pin turns of the gravel road to approach the Baralacha La (4,950 metres). Surrounded by 12 snow-laden mountain peaks, including Nunkun – the highest peak in Ladakh – this pass is a junction with a trekking and mule/yak path which leads southeast down into the Chandra valley and onwards into Spiti. On the north lies Lake Yunan Tso.

With these peaks for company, the road guides me to the wide-open spaces of Sarchu which has a few tents set up for weary travellers. But it is still early afternoon and I don't want to stop. I continue to ride ahead to the 21 Gata Loop road, which takes me heavenward rather quickly, ascending nearly 1,000 metres in just under eight kilometres. Again contrary to web grapevine, riding the 21 Gata Loops is also quite easy; the curves sharp but safe. I stop to take some photographs.

I feel none of the dreaded symptoms of high altitude sickness. My head feels as clear as it normally does (which is not saying much). Yesterday at Darcha, I'd had the contraindicated two drinks of rum but I am happily free of any undesirable repercussions – no nausea. I stretch my good fortune and light a celebratory cigarette.

The rocky red landscape around me could very well be on some other planet. Everything around me looks unworldly. No trees; not even shrubs. The few sparse patches of tiny violet gentians that grew near the river in Darcha were the last of any kind of vegetation I've seen today.

The nature of the ride has changed completely since the Rohtang Pass. Until then the traffic, the people and the habitation along the road have kept the brain concentrated almost fully on keeping the body alive. In the plains, the senses are constantly stimulated to the extreme. It is as if the entire country is on the streets. Rich men. Poor men. Village women working everywhere. Drunk truckers. Angry men, happy men. Beggars of all shapes, sizes and disabilities. Joyful faces, 'poor me' faces, resigned faces, hope-filled ones too. Children - always happy. Playing cricket with planks of wood for bats and dried coconuts for balls. The even poorer ones playing with just stones and bricks. And… Oh... yes… the noise! Blaring loudspeakers everywhere. Temples and mosques yelling out to a god in voices which are rarely sonorous. Festivities. Marriages. Funerals. Oh. India. How I love living here. What an alive country! So unpredictable. Where the poor are rich enough to welcome you into their huts and serve you food they themselves need. And the animals… cows strolling comfortably along all kinds of roads. How languidly they move, with the assurance of someone who is loved. Not even the most rash bus drivers would want to hurt them. Dogs. Donkeys. Horses. Camels. Elephants.

One might be riding solo but one is never alone. Not in the plains of India.

But now, amidst these arid mountains it is a different reality. The earth is not making any overtures to facilitate human habitation – the gritty, sandy soil offering no foothold to any tree. The heavy snows discouraging any kind of settlement.

Some time in the early afternoon, I have crossed from Himachal Pradesh into Ladakh.

Soon I am at the Lachlang La (5,065 metres) where I stop to soak in the silent scenery. The sun shines bright but it is still cold up here even at 3 o'clock in the afternoon. Unlike Baralacha La, where one is protected from the wind to a certain extent by the higher peaks of other mountains all around, here the unhindered breeze is strong and chilling and seems to penetrate into my head through my ears, nostrils and mouth.

As I cup my shivering palms to light my customary cigarette, I hear someone trudging up to the short stretch of flat surface that marks the peak. A woman who looks like she is around 25 years old, dressed in jeans and jacket, is walking towards me with sureness in her step and a smile on her face. For a while I am certain the altitude had altered my brain cells (they had warned me about this) but no, this spectre seemed packaged in flesh and skin and isn't transparent! 'Hi' it says.

'Hi' I answer automatically. She then says something, which really freaks me out.

'Aren't you Ajit?'

'Huh?' I am tempted to pinch myself to see if this is really happening.

'Surprised? I've seen your write-ups on the web with your photograph on the bike. Same guy right?'

To my, 'How come I didn't see you?' she says she'd been taking in the view from behind a boulder and perhaps that was why I had missed spotting her.

'I'm Farzana.'

Farzana and her husband, Irfan, are on a smaller 100 cc bike and she has had to walk up the steep road to relieve the load on the over-burdened engine. Irfan soon chuggs towards us with his machine trailing thick white smoke. His motorcycle is burning up too much oil. He parks his bike and comes towards us with two cameras hanging from his neck. Finally I have someone to take a photograph with me in it. I ask Farzana to come join me and get her to hug me and smile a genuinely fake grin – just for the photograph.

We all sit down on a nearby rock. They have another friend travelling with them, Trevor, who is on his bike and has gone ahead. Irfan tells me he is a free-lance photographer currently on assignment for a adventure travel magazine. He also teaches at a private college in Delhi. Farzana works for an advertising agency. Trevor, she said, is a sculptor. I would meet him in Pang where we all plan to halt for the night.

Pang, about halfway on the Manali-Leh road, is a flat open area, the size of four football fields. The mountains of rock and sand, which stand in front of us, have been chiselled by wind and snow into surrealistic shapes and I feel like I'm in an amphitheatre and huge beings with sandy faces are watching me. The wind blows in strong gusts.

There are four tent hotels, each of which is large enough to accommodate ten to 15 people. As in Darcha, the inside of the tent we enter is partitioned off into three sections – an eating area, the sleeping room for guests and the living quarters for the management. Irfan, Farzana, Trevor and I plonk down on the mattresses that are laid out on the floor in the dining area. Trevor is about 30. Thin, almost bony. His chin sports a trim triangular beard. He is from Kerala. He doesn't say much but when he does speak, he has a soft, gentle voice. Actually, none of us is in a mood for conversation. I, for one, am fatigued to the bone. Older bodies get tired earlier and then take longer to recover.

The two Tibetan women who are in charge here get busy preparing a meal for us (the inevitable *dal*-rice special). Simultaneously, they are taking care of a smiling chubby one-year-old who could have belonged to either of them. The baby is a loving presence in that tent. It sticks out its legs and its arms and chuckles with delight when Farzana picks him up. It was a boy! One of the ladies takes the baby from her and begins to lull him into sleep by singing a song. Her voice is soothing and very soft. At times it fades almost to a whisper.

The verses have the undulating rhythm typical of mountain music.

Again, as the sun goes down, the night fills up with stars which are so bright – they appear to be dollops of light just hanging around, beaming. The moon is on the rise and soon drowns the stars out to reign over the night sky. None of my three friends accept my offer of a drink and I alone am left to raise a toast to the cosmic glory that engulfs us this magical night.

When I awaken the next morning, my roommates are still asleep. Loading and securing my bags is by now an oft-repeated, streamlined operation, and with just one cup of tea in my belly, no breakfast, I am on the road climbing towards Tanglang La, the highest pass on the Manali-Leh road. It is only 6:30 a.m. The road is covered with a layer of sand and seems to hold to a perpetual 30-degree incline. Every view on every side is spectacular and I have to, I just have to stop and take a few pictures. Now this is not a simple a task. Especially as I decide not to get off the bike. There is no flat land to put it on its stand anyway. I stop close to the left edge of the road and put both my feet down to steady the bike. Pang now lies far below me. I must have already climbed a further 1,000 metres. The four tents look tiny and the river behind them just a thread of silver glittering in the morning sun.

I have developed a procedure for taking pictures from the saddle. Unzip the upper part of my high-altitude jacket. Take off my gloves and tuck them inside to prevent them from being blown away in the strong breeze which has been a constant feature on this road. Open the visor. Take off sunglasses and tuck them into front pocket. Take off helmet and balance it on the right rear view mirror. Then unzip another pocket and take out the small digital camera. Unfurl its crinkly plastic cover and put this along with the camera pouch inside the now bulging jacket. Then, make sure the camera-strap is around my wrist, steady myself and start looking through the viewfinder to frame the picture.

This time it almost doesn't work.

My left shoe slips on the loose gravel and I almost lose my balance. It is an instant of panic - a scary moment. But I manage to clamp on the front brake with my right hand. The bike skids a bit, then steadies. I am aware I could have plunged down on to the rocks below with bike and baggage and I try and look away from the deep drop on my left. I've just escaped becoming one more story in Vir Singh's police files. I try and calm myself and when my heart had returned to its normal rate of pulsations, take two pictures and put away the camera, don my sun-glasses, helmet and gloves and am on my way to Tanglang La.

First there are the Morey Plains to cross.

The road is arrow straight on a wide tableland between two mountain ranges with broad stretches of sand on either side. The high Tanglang is visible towards the north. I feel like a speck in this grand landscape where things change by the minute. One minute it is bright and sunny. And then a large grey cloud hides the sun.

Then the sand begins to whirl itself into tall thin dust devils over 50 feet high that have a life of their own, moving around briskly, maybe by some intelligent design.

In retrospect it was a miraculous sight but this morning I am overwhelmed by the scale of the strangeness all around me. My senses are saturated with awe.

The dust devils have run away from me and now a snow cloud begins to form up ahead. It approaches rather quickly. I am covered with wispy light snowflakes which melt almost as soon as they land on me.

Midway through, after an hour on the road, I see a lone Tibetan man, dressed in a maroon gown, sitting all by himself by the roadside. Probably a shepherd, but there are no sheep in sight. I am in no mood to stop and chat. The gravel road has now become lined with snow, stretching endlessly in front of me leading to the range of high mountains I will soon have to ascend.

I'm now in one of the highest deserts on earth. If the Google Earth satellite is looking at this area, the camera would catch a lone motorcyclist moving towards the peaks at a steady 30 kilometres per hour.

Gradually, the road becomes a roller coaster; begins to undulate as if it were a wave in the ocean. Up, up, up and then all the way down to a nallah, and then up again.

The incline is now getting serious. The road frequently loses its tar cover and becomes dusty. Fine desert dust gets into my eyes, nostrils, ears and every other place it can. There are small rocks strewn all over the surface, which means I have to slow down and avoid going over them.

Ahead I see two figures standing on the road next to an Enfield, which is parked by the side. As I approach them, one of them gestures for me to stop.

I pull up and get off the bike, divest myself of my headgear and look at two guys who are obviously also riding to Leh. They must both be in their late twenties and I guess they are from somewhere in Europe. After we've greeted each other with a 'hey', a 'hi' and a 'hello', I discover that they are Israelis and have been motorcycling northwards from New Delhi but have been stuck in this wilderness for the last two hours because the rear wheel of their bike is punctured. Do I have a spare tube? I've been carrying two extra tubes and pull out the one I've squeezed into a cavity under the seat. They want to know how much money I want for it. I tell them they can buy me a *chai* if we chance to meet again. This puts them in good humour and they begin to replace the punctured tube. They tell me they've both just finished the two years army training which is mandatory for everyone in Israel. Yoni has represented his country at the last Olympics in long jump. He tells me this when I ask him what he does in Israel. He says he's into fulltime, government-financed training for the next games.

The second one, who looks a few years older than Yoni, is David. He is an engineer and works for a company developing laser equipment used by beauty salons for the removal of unwanted hair. After they finish fitting the tyre back on, I loan them my foot pump to inflate the tube. Then I remount my steed and on my way I am.

It's been snowing lightly all this while. Frequently wiping the visor of my helmet with my gloved hands, I slow my pace and creep up the now narrowing road. At a point, I get a panoramic view of what lies ahead. Snow-laden mountains spread out all around as far as the eye can see. The road, a thin line hugging the mountain ahead of me, winding on and on towards what I presume must be Tanglang La (5,360 metres). From this distance, the majestic peak stands tall, like a monarch wearing a crown of white.

A military convoy of ten trucks loaded with supplies crawls ahead of me but the unpaved road is too narrow for me to overtake them and I crawl behind them for over an hour before the road widens just enough for me to pass.

When I finally reach T-Top, it is 11:30 in the morning. The Department of Digestion is reporting it has run out of biomass and needs a fresh intake. It feels good to be alive enough for this to be happening. I've not felt the pangs of hunger for decades. Here, on the second-highest motorable road in the world, I can only think of food – even the *dal*-rice combo would be welcome.

The flattish half-acre that is T-Top is laden with snow. In the centre is a two-foot high circular platform of concrete, painted in foot-wide striations of yellow and black. A concrete pyramid adorned with flags announces: YOU HAVE REACHED TANGLANG LA. Two other structures, both small rooms of concrete with asbestos roofs stand separated by a heap of freshly fallen, brilliant, white snow. One is a temple festooned with tiny yellow, red, orange and green triangular plastic flags. The other houses the *jawans* posted here to oversee the needs of the convoys that pass through on their way to Leh. A soldier walks up and we greet and ask each other standard questions.

I ask him to take my photograph and then hop on to the concrete platform and strike a nonchalant pose.

But my body is craving for nutrition and there is no food to be found here. The soldier tells me I'll get lunch at Rumtze which is only 30 minutes away. I begin to fantasizing about some fragrant mutton *biryani* as I ride down the steep incline into Rumtze, a small habitation, which marks the beginning of Central Ladakh.

My first meal of the day at a small Tibetan *dhaba* is again nothing other than my nemesis, but today I am not complaining. There is anyway no one to complain to. My mobile phone lies marooned in my jacket, far away from any BSNL tower, which could connect me to kith and kin and enable me to get any kind of payback on all this suffering I'm going through. I feel like a frustrated martyr. But I comfort myself with the thought that my immediate destination is not too far away. I am closing in on Leh.

Lazing Around Leh

After Rumtze, the ride becomes easy. I have reached the higher plains of Ladakh. Upshi is 60 kilometres away and Leh another 50, but it is all a well maintained, flat road and the journey is a breeze.

5 p.m. and I enter the capital city of Ladakh.

Wide concrete roads. Fields. Monasteries. Shops. Restaurants. Schools. Civilization.

I have reached Leh. (3,520 metres).

Another set of cosmic rules seems to apply here. The Buddhist denizens of Leh seem to be at peace with themselves and the world around them. Ancient faces etched with history glide by, whirling the Tibetan prayer wheel, lost in their private Shangri La.

Friendliness is in the air and smiles are easy to come by but hotels are not. Leh is packed with tourists from all over the world. Absolutely nowhere to stay. Unless, as one hotel manager tells me, I am ready to shell out Rs. 3,000 for a day's stay. I'm not. That's way over my budget. I walk to a nearby restaurant and ponder over my situation sipping a cup of some *kadak chai*.

My mobile still doesn't work so I walk up to an STD booth and call up an old pal of mine who is now a Brigadier in the Indian Army, posted in New Delhi. Soma, always an example of quick action, asks me to call him after half an hour and when I do, he has arranged for me to stay at the officers' mess of the MES at the Air Force Station. 'Go meet Major Dharmendar Singh, who will take care of you,' are his reassuring words. I ride westwards towards the airport.

The Officers' Mess is a row of six rooms connected by a narrow enclosed corridor. The aforementioned Major is helpful as anticipated and has got a room ready for me. I am escorted there by a young orderly who also carries my saddle-bags.

Ah! The luxury of a hot bath.

And there is a broad, clean bed to sleep on. The mess orderly assures me the dinner won't be *dal*-rice tonight. Would I like mutton *biryani*? I say 'Sure. But how about some Old Monk first?'

Life feels good these first hours in Leh, where the evening stays lit – first by the slow fading sunlight and then by the emerging moonlight which filters in through the window of the warm, insulated room. Seems like a lifetime ago that I was in 'big city' Manali.

I can actually feel the stress draining out from my muscles.

I drift into a state of blissful delirium.

I am a river flowing past forests and mountains.

I am the wind sweeping through snow-laden peaks.

I am silence.

I am… asleep.

When I wake up early next morning, I feel like a king. I know I'm indulging myself in self-pleasure as I let my mind run free, unhindered by any restraint of modesty. The three days I've been traversing the Manali-Leh sector seem like a compartmentalized lifetime apart. I realize that had I known how rough and tough this stretch is, I would not have undertaken to do it alone. In spite of my mechanic Ramesh's short-term training programme, I was still an almost total nincompoop when it came to diagnosing and correcting the motorcycle's mechanical problems and so many things could have gone wrong.

But the fact that I hadn't felt a bit of high altitude sickness; that the bike and I had survived the crater-studded road over five high mountain passes; all this now appears as something that would not have been possible without divine grace. I had foolishly challenged common sense and had two drinks of rum in Darcha and Pang. Contrary to medical advice, not only had I stayed for more than the recommended five minutes but had also smoked a self-congratulatory cigarette as I stood enthralled on each mountain top. Perhaps even at the best of altitudes my lungs are not used to oxygen and the rarefied air hasn't bothered me.

Why do we all imagine God resides somewhere upwards? Because that is where I raise my eyes and say a prayer of silent thanks to the Almighty to have allowed me to indulge in my playful foolishness that prompted this journey in the first place. I am still fatigued and would like nothing better than to sleep all day long but today is June 28, the last day of the Hemis festival – my first and last chance to witness what promises to be an unusual sight.

So with a hearty Services' breakfast tucked under my belt, I kick-start the now unloaded Enfield into action. Karu is only 30 kilometres away and the ride is nice and easy. From Karu the road climbs up for ten kilometres snaking over smaller hills and lo.. *–aaa gaya Hemis*.

Set in the midst of mountains with the city of Leh a misty presence near the horizon, Hemis is home to the most important ancient Buddhist monastery.

Established in 1672 AD, Hemis monastery is famous for its colourful annual festival which is held on the tenth day of the fifth lunar month (June/July) to celebrate the birth of their founder Padmasambhava. Every twelve years, in the year of the monkey, the festival is considered especially auspicious. One of the big attractions is the 62-feet-long silk and gold scroll, richly embroidered with pearls and precious stones, the *thangka,* displayed only every twelve years. Today is that day.

Everyone is in Hemis today, and why not? This is what they have come to Leh for. It takes some time to find parking even for a motorcycle – all available space is packed with vehicles – buses, SUVs, private cars and motorcycles. Hundreds of people, over half of them foreigners, are converging towards a large courtyard in front of the monastery. Buddhists have come from all over Ladakh, dressed in their finest traditional garments. Stalls selling Buddhist artefacts line both sides of the road. There are more stalls in another area and that is where I first go. Most are run by Tibetan women who are selling prayer wheels of varying sizes, flutes, bells, brass replicas of monasteries, bead and silver jewellery, chimes, wooden mortars and pestles and ornate small and large boxes looking antique enough to store even the Da Vinci code. The plump woman sitting on a cushion amidst her wares is glad to sell me my selection. I now have a few necklaces, earrings, rings and such to take back for my friends.

An adjacent area seems reserved for cooking. I can smell the fragrance of burning deodar. Two young saffron-clad monks are stirring curry in a huge pot placed over a blazing fire. Each has a long-handled ladle which they are also using as a musical instrument. Around the pot they go, chanting a song in unison and punctuating the completion of each short verse with three rapid clicks of their ladles. After watching them for a while, I walk into the large open courtyard of the three storey high Hemis *gompa* where over a thousand people have collected. Colour – rust and red and yellow and green. Tall poles with flags spear the blue sky. The precious *thangka* is hanging on the monastery wall and there is a crowd of people staring up at it and taking photographs. Many visitors have found seats while others stand, waiting around an empty square where the show is stated to begin soon. Several cameras are on the ready for the main event. Presently, a group of ten masked lamas enter the arena. They represent the various Tibetan gods of the Dugpa order. Two of them are carrying large drums and stand by the side, while the others take positions around the central pole. The lamas are wearing long, ornately brocaded gowns and quaint black hats. High-pitched yells suddenly rent the air as the dance begins. They are enacting one of the numerous stories from the ancient Buddhist texts, sacred plays called *chhams*. Cymbals, drums and long horns – all contribute to the drama as the lamas prance about while the enthused camera owners in the audience jostle for space to take photographs.

These dances represent the triumph of good over evil and end with the ritual sacrifice of a human figure made of dough, accompanied by even louder shrieks.

The enactments continue through the afternoon.

The sun blazes away in ultraviolet glory. The skin of my face and arms resembles burnt toast, well beyond reaping the benefits of skin lotions offering UV-protection. These creams only make me look like burnt toast with lots of butter on it. Actually, I am looking forward to be seen as a sunburnt mountaineer when I return home. That should surely impress the ladies! I decide to let my skin burn as I wend my way back to my waiting bike only to see another Enfield parked next to it, which looks exactly like Yoni and David's. And sure enough, I see them walking towards me, broad smiles on their faces.

Yoni says they owe me a cup of tea and we go to one of the stalls near the parking lot and sit and chit-chat about our bikes and the Manali-Leh road. David says he suffered from nausea and severe headache at Tanglang La and had to use the oxygen cylinder they've brought with them from Israel. He looks fine now. Yoni tells me they plan to return to Manali and from there to Dharamshala. Later, they plan to take their bike all the way south to Goa where they would spend the winter. I tell them they can stay with me if they are going via Pune and David writes down my address in the diary he's pulled out of his jacket.

I thank them for the tea, say goodbye and get on the bike to roll down to the main road, which will take me back to my luxurious lodgings at the Air Force Officers' Mess.

Along the way I accost groups of saffron-clad children who splash water at passers-by and yell '*Joley*' every time they hit their target, which right now is me! I figure this must be something like our own *Holi* festival where we sprinkle colour on each other. The faces of these children are all full of mirth and mischief. Each has a plastic bucket full of plain, uncoloured water by his side and a mug full of it in his hands. They are ready for me.

It is quite cold and I really don't want to get wet, so I zip past these 'Denis the Menaces' and speed on.

It is early evening as I park outside my room at the Officers' Mess. The sun is losing its sway over Leh and the ever-waiting cold starts to reassert its hold. The white-walled Mess is lit in soft gold. Two of the other rooms are occupied. I spot two men sitting in the porch, sunning themselves. They must be my neighbours, so I walk over there to say hello. They are both in their late forties.

One is a supplier of corrugated fibreglass and has come all the way from Bangalore. He tells me he is not at all enamoured by the location because of the breathing difficulty he has at this altitude. His face has an ashen pallor and he looks distinctly uncomfortable. He cannot understand why I am travelling the way I am and although he is a decade younger than me, I sense a tinge of fatherliness in his manner. He introduces me to the other guest who is also a contractor but involved with road building.

We sit together for a while and then the cold forces us to return to our heated rooms. They invite me for a drink but I excuse myself on grounds of fatigue. I really don't fancy an evening discussing disease, inflation, profits and other such matters.

A day passes and then another.

Walking around downtown, eating exotic meals by the roadside, visiting the *gompas* scattered all around, I savour the aroma of this ancient city, where the very air feels different. I wonder if the lack of oxygen is making everyone feel light-headed?

The pavements of the main street are crowded with travellers from foreign lands. So is the café I've stopped at for a cup of cappuccino. I'm sitting at a corner table on a porch overlooking the road, my attention occupied by the scene below me. There are the older locals, dressed in traditional Tibetan dress, a long red and rust cloak flowing all the way to the feet, which are shod in heavy mountain shoes made of thick leather and festooned with at least a bit of red. Many wear the pagoda-like raised hat lined with thick fur on the inside. There are some very old folk walking around here, several whirling a portable prayer wheel. Their faces etched with deep furrows and the skin burnt a dark brown, they look ancient and knowledgeable and kind; as if they are above the mundane wheeling and dealing that is going on all around them. The younger generation favours jeans and jackets. Many of these young locals are involved with the tourist trade and this is the height of the tourist season, probably the only few months they have to make some money.

'Ess this chair taken?' a voice interrupts my reverie and I look up to see a young white girl with short golden hair, laden with a huge, blue backpack, which she is in the process of unloading from her shoulders.

'No. You can take it,' I answer in a voice tinged with a suggestion that she was welcome to sit there with me. I am thirsting for some company and she looks prime time.

'Can I sit here?' She asks again.

'Sure.'

We sit in silence for a while and then when the waiter brings me my coffee, she says 'That looks good,' and orders one for herself.

'You look like you have come a long way,' I say and she smiles and says, 'Yes.' She's from Germany and travelling on her own. She has just come into Leh on the flight from Delhi. Has been in India for a month, travelling through Rajasthan and she's fallen in love with India. Her name is Ingrid.

Wasn't that the name of my patient, Jeremy D'Costa's girlfriend too? I look up at the sky and sure enough, there he is in the clouds, smiling his typical benign smile.

'Your country is so diverse, so big. Germany is so small,' Ingrid says. I agree and put in my own two-bits worth of promotion for Indian tourism.

She is interested when I tell her I've come on a motorcycle.

Afterwards, we walk to where my bike is parked and she looks at the machine and asks enthusiastic questions about it. When I tell her that I am planning to ride to Nubra valley, she asks if she can ride with me.

The villages of Deskit and Hunder are as close to Siachen as a civilian can get and a special permit is needed from the commissioner of Leh to enter them. His office is a kilometre away and I ride towards it with Ingrid sitting easily balanced on the rear seat.

The commissioner's office is part of a larger complex

towards the edge of the crowded market area and we enter a small room lined with open steel shelves, packed with bundles of documents wrapped in their files and tied with pieces of string. The deputy commissioner turns up after only a ten-minute wait and when we tell him we need permits to go to Nubra valley, he says he'll issue me a permit without any problem. Citizens of India merely need to make an application on plain paper. Ingrid can only travel in a group with at least three other foreigners. I tell him I'll vouch for her. 'But who will vouch for you?' he replies with a twinkle in his eye. Wow. A bureaucrat with a sense of humour! Ingrid is disappointed but a young local who has been loitering within earshot approaches her and says he can get her in with a group of New Zealanders who are travelling in an SUV and she follows him out of the room, telling me she'll wait for me outside the office. Later, I say *tschuess* to her over a cup of sweet Ladakhi tea from a nearby roadside stall and return to the Air Force Station located far from the main city.

The Magical Mountain

Awake at 5 a.m. These last three days of sedentary living and good eating has relaxed body and mind and I am anxious to get going. But today I need not hurry. My destination for the day is only 120 kilometres away and even on bad roads, even if I go at snail's pace, this should not take more than six hours.

I have a breakfast of *parathas* and *bhujiya*, topped with the all-important two cups of thick tea, after which I am ready to take off on my northward journey. The road I've taken out of Leh is unmarked and I want to make sure I'm headed the right way. It's just about dawn and there is no one on the road who could confirm my direction. The sun is only a glow behind the mountains to my right and I know I'm going northwards. Along the way, half a kilometre off the road, is a small hut and I spot two tribal women and a young boy standing around what appears to be an open cemented tank with water in it. A mother, her teenage daughter and 10 year old son are washing their faces. They are dressed in layers of sheep skin which makes them look like actors in a Ghengis Khan movie. Smoke rises from a smouldering fire nearby.

I guide the bike over the dusty pathway towards this habitation and the three figures freeze all action and look at me with surprise. I stop and remove my helmet. The surprised expression on their face doesn't abate. I ask them if the road goes to Khardung La? I have to repeat my question three times before they understand what I am saying. Then the older woman raises her right arm and points in the direction I was going. I smile my thanks, re-don my helmet and kick start the motorcycle. I can see they are visibly relieved to watch me go. I wonder what makes these mountain folk so wary of outsiders. Surely, they have seen many motorcyclists on this road?

First in patches and soon in unbroken lines, the road becomes edged with snow, glowing in the morning sunlight. But the centre of the road is well-maintained with not a pothole in sight. Within the hour, I have reached the South Puli check post, located at the base of Khardung La.

The check post is a group of brick walled and tin roofed offices where officious looking sentries stop vehicles to check papers and permits. There is a canteen and further down, away from everything else, are the toilets. I show my permit and get it stamped, have tea at the canteen, use the toilet and then I'm on my way. The climb suddenly becomes steep. The Enfield purrs on effortlessly. I love the sound of a happy engine. Soon I find myself on the top of the world.

So this was the famous Khardung La. (5,602 metres). The highest motorable road in the world according to some claims. Other surveys say it is actually the nearby Marsmik which deserves that position.

I park the bike and look around. It is a spectacular sight. Towards the north are high mountains as far back as the eye can see.

Lesser peaks play peek-a-boo around the white clouds, which hang below us. All peaks are covered with snow. Khardung towers over its neighbours and the valleys around it are deep. I've been looking at a pair of vultures swirling down towards a collection of rocks on a smaller mountain. It is a rare enough sight to spot even scavenging birds here. These look like high fliers and I wonder what altitudes they cruise at. All around me are rocks of various colours. From pitch black through various shades of brown, to vivid patches of dark green, blue and also yellow and white. But there is no vegetation here. The breeze has no leaves to rustle through, so it uses the crevices between rocks and snow to create the universal sound of 'OM', which seems to reverberate all around me. Awed reverence is all I feel. Maybe I've been reading too much of the 'new age' stuff and am psyching myself into forced spiritual awareness; and maybe to someone else who came here, the wind would sound like a demon's shriek or even a banshee's wail, but all I hear is 'OM'. Didn't someone say that there are as many worlds as there are people? That each of us perceives the same reality differently?

I close my dazzled eyes, but the sun still shines through my eyelids and plunges me into a sea of deep red. Some micro-particles of the sand in my eyes form whirlpools of black that flit about in spurts and jerks in their thick liquid world. Suddenly… a strong chilling breeze is blowing my gloves away and I sprint from my seat and manage to catch them before they fly out of reach.

In a moment of affection, I touch the chilled metal tank of my bike and whisper a 'thank you'. I cast a furtive look around. Three soldiers are sunning themselves near by and I don't want them to hear me talking to a motorcycle, because by this time, my unshaven scraggly face looks unkempt and a first impression may not inspire an onlooker's confidence about my absolute sanity!

I feel fine. No HAPE, even here. But I don't want to stay too much longer than the maximum ten minutes recommended by doctors. Better to play it safe.

As I descend on to the northern side of Khardung La towards Nubra valley, the road suddenly becomes hazardous. Its cover of tar has been washed away and boulders of various sizes sit strewn all over my path. There is water everywhere. It's too early in the day for the bigger snows to melt, but it's already warm enough for the process to have started, as I carefully splash through six inches of flowing water, afraid to raise my feet too high in case the bike slips, but not really wanting to get my shoes wet either. Ninety minutes (22 kilometres) of this focused riding fatigues mind and body and when the tar road reappears, I am glad to stop and get off to flex my stiff legs and stretch my arms wide. Someone else seeing me might think I was trying to embrace the Himalayas. A dark brown, jagged mountain peak lurks next to where I'm standing. I'm glad its only early afternoon and sunny bright. The same sight would be foreboding in a darkened sky. The clutch cable needs adjustment – it has worked overtime the last hour and a half. My short course in motorcycle maintenance comes in handy and soon I am on the go again.

The village of Khalsar appears just around one of the numerous bends and I stop at a *dhaba* for lunch. The menu… you guessed it… but I had to eat it! If I die today, they'll find me stuffed with *dal* and rice. As if in compensation, I have company for lunch. They're a young, white couple who walk in and stop and look around for a place. There is only one table and they have little choice but to come and sit across from me.

I can't figure out how they've managed to look so sparkling clean while my own face resembles burnt bread, which has been kneaded with dirt and grease.

We smile and greet each other.

'Hi.'

'Hi.'

They tell the waiter they want two *thalis* of the house speciality.

She's Helen and he's Tom.

'Both of you look so unsoiled,' I finally have to say.

Tom tells me they've just spent two hours under a nearby waterfall and encourages me to do the same. But… brrrr… an icy glacial water bath doesn't hold great appeal for me. 'You look like you need a bath,' he chuckles.

'I was a white guy when I started the journey from Pune,' I say and this feeble attempt at humour is rewarded by a bright sparkling smile from Helen. She is beautiful. Her shoulder-length blonde hair, wet now, highlights the tan of her face and tiny diamond ear studs throw intermittent beams of reflected sunlight into my eyes. I try and filter out desire from my mind and glance at her with a mellow look that encourages her to continue her conversation with me, while Tom eats his rice and *dal*. She is telling me about the countryside of her native England where she's headed after having spent three years teaching in an Australian school. I must have said something ridiculous or funny because there she goes flashing her brilliant smile again… Whoosh…

Older hearts are known to tumble to lighter bait.

And I realize mine has got hit in an unexpected ambush. For the 21 days that I've been riding, I've kept myself entertained in a self-sufficient kind of way. I have had numerous conversations with myself, sung aloud many songs inside the dark bubble of my helmet, crooned out to lovers past and lost and lately, I've been romancing with the gods. But now I am empty of all internal dialogue.

Memories of past events lose their allure with each progressive repetition and I'm thirsting for some stimulating new thoughts. Helen and Tom have provided me with this much-needed social interlude. After they ride back towards Leh, I miss their vibrancy and feel even more isolated.

I am near the extreme northern border of India. Siachen is not too far away. But the limitations imposed by the Ladakh commissioner's permit prompt me away from the large steel bridge which leads to Siachen. I have access to the Nubra valley villages of Deskit and Hunder. I'm planning to stop for the night in Hunder.

The valley of Nubra, with its grassy meadows and its varieties of fruit and other trees, is one of the few fertile green places here, almost flaunting its beauty to a generally arid Ladakh. A river meanders in a shallow delta over sands of the most vibrant shades. Emerald greens merge with sunflower yellow only to turn subtle pink.

Is there no end to the magic of the Master Weaver?

I've been riding long enough and the motorcycle feels like an extension of my body. The mind is free to wander. Spread out over a few hectares on my right, I pass large breast-shaped sand dunes. On my left are jagged pinnacles of snow-crowned rock and the dunes appear incongruous partners in this high Himalayan locale. My thoughts are stuck on Radio Woman FM. 'Hey, old man, where have all your lovers gone?' Helen's smiling countenance mocks me from behind one of the dunes and then disappears. A bout of melancholy catches hold of me. Often in the past, when such moods have struck, I've tried pretending they didn't exist and indulged in cover-up operations. Such procedures have never worked for me so now the evolved strategy is to just let it be. Enjoy it, even.

'Doctor, I feel quite fatigued these days,' says a middle-aged man to his physician who advises him to cut his sex life in half. 'Which half Doc,' questions the patient, 'thinking about it or talking about it?'

I'm playing mind games now, trying to distract my depression away, but I know it is going to take its time leaving and I have to allow it that time. It cannot be rushed out of the psyche with any hint of force. That would only feed it with a kinetic kind of energy, which would replenish its power and delay its departure. Have to flow unresisting in this current and let it take me where it will.

I think I'm going crazy.

I am travelling back in time on a magic raft, flowing past a Californian forest where it is early morning, and the blue tent I set up the evening before has a translucent sheen to it, with the rising sun as its backdrop. It half-hides Diane from my view but I know she's sleeping inside. Soon, the light brightens and I can see her silhouette shift position.

'Hi Jay,' her sleepy soft voice calls me by my other name. I savour these remembered delights and try to hold them in my mind's eye for a while longer. The memories take on a nostalgic delight. Almost as if I were a voyeur, peeping in on someone else. That was a different me then.

I have reached the northernmost point of my journey and as I enter the picturesque village of Hunder, my mileage-meter tells me that I am 3,500 kilometres from home. All around in Hunder, I see green. There are small orchards thick with vegetation. There are irrigation canals which bring clear, icy water from the glaciers nearby. I roam through its narrow cobbled alleys for over two hours looking for accommodation but without success. The few places which take in travellers, are all booked. A couple of women are carrying hay back to their farm and as I stop to ask them for help in finding a place to stay overnight in their exquisite village, they smile revealing darkened dentitions. What must they chew here? Their teeth are a cosmetic dentist's delight. And they, in turn look at me as if I had dropped in on Hunder in a flying saucer. I must look a sight too. I ask them about a hotel again and this time the stacks of hay they're carrying on their heads move left and right as they nod me a twin negative and walk away.

Eventually, I spot a farmer standing near the rickety gate of his farm, almost as if he was waiting for me. I ask him if he can put me up for one night. He nods 'yes' without a moment's delay and then escorts me up a stairway to the room I was to occupy. By mountain standards, it was a large room. The wooden floor was thickly carpeted and the walls adorned with colourful tapestries of Buddhist images. I like this room. It feels warm and welcoming. Tsering Motup is the farmer's name and he looks older than his 40 years. The extreme cold and the brilliant sunlight have burnt his skin dark brown and a hood of thickened skin protects his eyes like an awning. His Hindi is good enough for an exchange of basic introductions. But he is surprisingly non-inquisitive about me. Perhaps he thinks I'm some kind of army spy? Or even an enemy agent? I remind myself that this is after all, the state of Jammu and Kashmir. He doesn't ask me where I'm from or anything else but I have many questions for him.

Tsering tells me his family is away attending the celebrations in Hemis, which is why he could let me use this room.

And how does he make his living?

For a few months every year, Tsering finds work carting loads up the Siachen glacier to keep the soldiers supplied with the necessities of survival. He walks in a group of five men who carry loads of up to 80 kilograms each, over altitudes above 6,000 metres. He makes enough money on these trips to last him the entire year. His farm provides the vegetables his family needs. He got his own land when his father divided his land between his sons. The adjacent properties belong to his brother. He smiles and says he has good land.

He doesn't need to tell me he also has a cow. I can smell her, parked as she is right under the window. A horde of flies buzzes around me.

It's the first day of July and the early moon is a large ball of gold which hangs limpidly over the tranquil valley. Night falls quickly in Hunder. Even though it is cold, I prefer to sit out under the canopy of the lit sky. I have to cover myself in layers of warm clothes.

Two soldiers climb up the staircase towards where I sit. One has a bottle of rum in his hands. They're talking with each other in Marathi. '*Vikaaychi ahe ka*?' (Want to sell it?), I ask them in the same language and both instantly have a surprised grin on their faces. '*Marathi bolta*?' (You speak Marathi?). I tell them I'm from Pune, They're both from Latur in Maharashtra. They tell me they are thrilled to hear me speaking Marathi. They give me the bottle of rum but refuse to take any money for it. They call me *apla Marathi manoos* (our Marathi man), wish me a safe journey. The sound of their heavy boots on the shaky wooden stairs brings Tsering out. He goes down with them and sees them to the gate.

Tonight, I shall filter the gold of the full moon through the amber of my glass. My gloved hands raise a toast to this golden eye in the night sky. Later, Tsering brings out the dinner he has cooked and we eat together. He's no great conversationalist and I'm in no mood to ask any more prying questions for tonight.

Yawn! How does one say 'good night' in Hunder? I am too weary to ask but two suppressed smiles are exchanged and Tsering goes into his room while I go to my bed.

The moonlight comes in through the thin curtains and highlights a face. At least one of the gods on the wall is watching as I slip into the half-sleep of the physically and emotionally fatigued.

I wake up to the sound of bovine mooing. Then hear Tsering singing an ode to his cow. The milk, which I later drink is naturally sweet, flavoured as it is with his song. I've had a dreamless sleep and feel recharged to some extent.

I go and sit on my aluminium chair in the open space outside the room. I take a deep breath of the fresh air and can feel it surge into each tiny pocket of my lungs. Sounds of gurgling water from the silvery three-feet-wide irrigation canal that borders Tsering's field are mixed with the low-pitched dang dang of the cow's wooden bell.

I close my eyes and sit silently, feel the cold breeze glide over my bare arms and my face. It tries to blow away the heavy sensations of yesterday but achieves only limited success. I am not quite out of my gloomy mood. An hour passes. The sun is up and burning my skin. I move inside and set camp on the bed that lies under the open window. From my first floor vantage, I look down at the activity below. Tsering, dressed in the brown pants and green sweater of his army-porter's uniform almost seems to merge with the cabbages growing in the green patch behind the cow shed. Butterflies! Birds! I'm seeing them after a lifetime. Small birds chirrup in the bushes that line the boundary of Tsering's property.

Later, when he brings me a cup of Ladakhi tea, I tell him I'll soon be on my way and begin to pack for my ride back to Leh. I ask him about the double-humped camels of Hunder which everyone has told me I must see and he explains where they are to be found.

The road to the camel farm is a flattened stretch but it is under construction. There are innumerable cricket-ball-sized rocks, so densely strewn all over, that I have a trying time balancing my loaded bike. It's footwork that keeps me from falling and ten minutes on this obstacle course is enough for me to decide to leave the camels where they are. I decide to lump them. In any case, watching something, which is 'double-humped' is hardly going to help me. In the state of mind I'm in, I have to be careful now even with the words I think about.

Turning around is a tricky manoeuvre. When I finally free myself from this road of shifting balls, I stop to realign mind and body to some semblance of functionality and get back on to the road to Leh.

Stuck in a Road River

As the day heats up, these mountain roads become inundated with glacier melt. I must reach the North Puli check post before 1 p.m. if I am to reach Leh by nightfall.

As I begin the steep upward climb, with snow packed on the roadside, I remember Juhi's reply when I had asked her what she wanted me to get for her from Ladakh. 'Bring me some snow, Baba', she'd said which had then reminded me of the Ramayana story where Prince Rama cried for the moon. His mother, the story goes, showed him a reflection of the moon in a saucer of water and the child-god was happy and stopped crying.

I stop and get off the bike. Picking up a sharp stone, I etch my daughter's name in large capital letters on the almost vertical wall of angel-white snow lining the road, then move back and take a picture of it. That should make her happy. I'm being a good father.

I need to hurry now. I must get across Khardung La within the next hour. And right until the moment trouble hit, I presumed that re-crossing Khardung La would be as easy as coming over it was yesterday morning. But today the same road looks and feels different. Yesterday, it had been morning when I crested the Khardung La. Today, it is past noon and the sun has had enough time to start melting the ice caps that crown the peaks.

Across a sharp bend, a torrent of frothy water is rushing over the road. Actually there is no 'road'. Only large boulders of polished white rocks over which flows a 'river' two feet deep. On my left was the crotch in the mountains from where water was gushing out with increasing vigour. The usable part of the road was about eight feet across and it then sloped down to a deep chasm on my right where the glacier melt plunged downwards in a waterfall. How deep was this chasm? I was afraid to look down. I should have kept the bike a couple of feet to my right where the boulders were smaller and would probably have made it across to the other side without much difficulty. But my fear of slipping off the edge makes me stay closer to the side of the mountains where the larger rocks are and I lunge into the current with my loaded bike to get stuck almost immediately.

Swearing is allowed when there is no one else to

hear it and I let out a yell any yeti would have been proud of. But that doesn't help. I stay stuck.

The rear wheel is embedded in a foot-deep pothole and the front wheel is locked between two large white rocks. This looks like it's going to be serious.

I am immobilized. I can't nudge my bike by even an inch. It is impossible to get off because the bike can't be put on its stand, what with those shifting rocks under it. So there I sit, with nothing to do but muse on the state of my current affairs. I shouldn't have forgotten to cover my socks with plastic bags before wearing my shoes, as I had done all through the trip so far. Within seconds my shoes, socks and feet are sopping wet.

My body begins to lose heat and the possibility of hypothermia becomes real. I realize that before long I'll have to let the bike fall and get myself out of this freezing water. But that would tilt the petrol tank and spill most of the precious fuel into the flowing water. I decide to just sit and wait for the issue to resolve itself. I think I am saved when I first hear a low rumble and then see a truck climbing towards me in low gear. But it doesn't stop to help me out. As the wheels of the loaded truck pass not six inches from me, the lone driver yells out that the truck's engine needs to be kept revved up or it would die and he didn't dare stop. Any hope of quick deliverance recedes with the diminishing sound of the truck's grinding gears as it turns around the bend ahead.

What could I do now? Pray? Wonderful idea! I close my eyes under the helmet and meditate on my soul mentor. Babaji! The ancient wizard appears in my visualization and smiles his blessings once again. This time he's in the green garb of the old Sufi I'd met near Pali. He transmits a simple message. 'Take off your helmet.' I open my eyes and do his bidding. How would taking my helmet off help me, I wonder? And what do I do with the helmet now? I need both my hands on the handle to keep the heavy bike upright. I hold the handle with my left hand for the three seconds it takes to toss the helmet across the waters where it lands with a metallic clang. Glad my head wasn't in it!

Presently, a genuine saviour arrives.

He comes in a new truck, which passes me and pulls up ahead of the patch of flowing water. He leaps down from his high driver's seat and walks towards me. He is bearded and dressed in the long *kurta* hanging over a loose *salwar*– the typical garb of Kashmiri men. He is about 25 years old. Without much more than a brief greeting, he comes to the bike, puts both his hands on the handle and pulls it up and out. I thank him and want to give him some money but he refuses to take it. Says it was my white hair that made him stop and help me. He seems to be in a hurry to leave and jumps into his truck and drives off before I can say anything.

Babaji's advice works in miraculous ways. Literally

out of a hole, the experience has left me with a gift. The knot of depression has been washed away in the cold road-river of Khardung La.

It's early evening and the sky looks an ominous grey as I park on K-Top for the second time. High altitude sickness is still on my mind. All through this trans-Himalayan journey, my body has been spared any suggestion of dizziness, vomiting or nausea. The marshal laws laid out in Pune have worked so far. But I don't want to push my luck. I must not stay on the pass for longer than five minutes. My only real discomfort is my wet shoes and wetter socks. I open my saddle-bags to get an old pair of shoes I'm carrying for just such an emergency and dig out a pair of woollen socks, which don't smell very nice but are warm and dry.

As I sit on a rock and change my footwear, I see two motorcycles approaching the top from the Leh side. They are still a distance away and look dwarfed by the high mountains around them. The sound of their bikes has the unmistakable Enfield beat which echoes off the rocks. Soon they too reach the top and dismount. When they take off their helmets, I can see the riders are young and white. I've now got my dry socks on and my feet feel the difference. I tie my shoelaces and walk over to them. I want a picture of me on K-Top and they are the only ones here. No soldiers in sight today.

Introductions are made.

Jack doesn't have to tell me he's American. His nasal twang takes me back to Lubbock, Texas. John says he's from London. I tell them I am surprised to see their bikes free of any luggage. Jack explains they have a vehicle following them, carrying their luggage, food and everything they need including a mechanic. Equipped against all odds. He sees my loaded bike and opines that I should travel lighter. I tell him I'm riding solo and doesn't he see I've no backup vehicle? We just take pictures of each other with our digital cameras and say our goodbyes. I've become emotionally numb.

The wind, a constant presence here, flutters the saffron and red plastic flags strung across poles of a nearby temple, waving a vigorous goodbye, spurring me to leave.

I make haste to begin the glide down towards Leh. The road after Khardung La is paved all the way. I stop again to have a cup of tea with the guards at the South Puli checkpoint. Soon I see the white tops of the *gompas*, which tell me I am on the outskirts of Leh.

This time, I decide not to return to the Officers' Mess. For one, it is located too far away from 'downtown' Leh. And comfortable though the facilities are, the distance effectively cuts me off from the local populace. I want to be able to mingle with the locals and do what they do. The guesthouse I've located is in the heart of downtown Leh and has a wonderful cook who can cook everything except *dal* and rice! Over the next two days,

I reacquaint myself with civilized living while keeping my body nourished with delicious food and drink.

I've been keeping a close eye on the motorcycle's performance; regularly replenishing spent engine oil and taking care of other basic maintenance. I still have about 700 kilometres to ride.

The Zoji La, which separates Ladakh from the Kashmir valley, is known to be difficult terrain to cross. The clutch, brake and accelerator cables might need to be replaced, as might the clutch plates and spark plug. I've got the spares but decide it would be best if I get the bike checked by an experienced mechanic. Everyone I ask tells me Juma is the only guy in Leh who understands the Enfield and he's not too hard to locate with a workshop right on the road to the airport. A crowd of onlookers has collected around his workshop and as I approach it, I am witness to a strange scene. A stocky middle-aged grease-smudged man is in an argument with one of his customers over costs of services rendered. The vehicle in question is unarguably the filthiest Enfield I have ever seen. The Royal Enfield is really a connoisseur's bike and is almost always kept in sparkling condition by its loving owner. The owner of this machine is another story.

He is about 25 years old. His shoulder-length hair is unkempt. He must have let many moons go since his last bath. His nails are black with grease and dirt, as is his face. Has he been living all by himself in a jungle?

His bike is rusty and I marvel at how bald the tyres are. A shabby, large black cotton bag is perched on a thick mattress placed across the rear seat, both tied with a rope.

I look on as the two graduate from verbal abuse to physical blows and I wonder if I want to do business with this establishment. Suddenly the customer rushes to his bike, kicks it into life, and moves out of the scene with a clumsy jerk. The other man, who I presume is Juma, walks towards me with his facial expression switched to its 'polite' mode. I tell him I'm on my way to Srinagar and ask if he can check my bike out. He nods confidently and I get off and park the bike. He then walks around it, testing the front brakes and the clutch, turns around and tells me everything 'looks all right'. I ask if he wants to ride the bike. He again nods a vigorous 'yes', gets astride and takes it for a two-minute spin. He returns and says everything is fine. When I ask him specific questions about the cables or the brake linings, all he says is, 'Trust in God,' which I think is a strange thing for a mechanic to say. He then demands a hundred rupees. Unsatisfied but without another option, I hand him his fee and ride back to my hotel. I still have to pack my saddle-bags and prepare for the long ride towards Srinagar the following morning. It is my last evening in Leh.

The Lamayuru Diamond

It's 6 o'clock in the morning and I've already covered 20 kilometres of the 450 that separate me from Srinagar. My destination today is Kargil, 200 kilometres away. If I reach Kargil before 4 p.m., I'll still have time to cover the 56 kilometres to Dras and then make that my night halt. It will be really good if I can reach Dras before dark. If I don't, I'll have to get up at 3 a.m. the next morning. But I'll worry about all that later. For now, it is this road I must focus on. The surface varies from the 'all right' to the 'cratered' kind and my average speed cannot exceed 35 kilometres per hour.

This stretch out of Leh is very sparsely inhabited with only a few fenced military encampments. Stopping by the wayside, I shell the two boiled eggs I told the cook to pack for me and share only a small piece with a wayside mongrel which has warily approached me, having smelled egg in the cold dry air. I wash down my breakfast with lots of water, flex my legs and arms and continue with the journey. A large monastery in the distance reflects the morning sunlight off its whitewashed exterior and seems to beckon me towards it. I stop near the base of the mountain and look up at the monastery, now towering over me, perched halfway up the mountainside on my right. Two young lamas with shaven scalps and dressed in maroon, who appear to have been waiting along the road, suddenly start waving their hands at me and then are smiling as they approach me.

'Welcome to Lamayuru,' one of them says. I am pleasantly surprised by this bonhomie from the normally staid Buddhists. 'We didn't know you were travelling on a motorcycle,' says the taller one and asks me where the others in the group were? It is soon obvious to them that they have mistaken me for someone else. This realization of their confusion makes them break down in peals of laughter followed by apologies. They urge me to visit Lamayuru.

'It's a powerful place for miracles,' the monks tell me. Sensing my interest, the taller one informs me that mysterious gifts come to those on whom these gods smile. Would I be one of the lucky blessed ones? I tell them I have to make it to Dras and cannot visit the monastery. For today's ride, daylight is at a precious premium. The monks nod and smile and stand aside. I get off the bike and looking up at the monastery, pay my homage from a distance. I ask the Lord Lamayuru to forgive me my bad manners and not withhold his bounty from me.

A miracle or two would sure be welcome.

The rough, mud-sloshed road now begins to demand attention. It winds its way through a lunar landscape. There are shards of sharp rock on this road and I have to prevent the Enfield from going over any of them. Their knife-like edges can slit even new tyres. I am riding along the banks of the river Indus. At a point, just before I enter the wayside village of Mulbekh, the mountains seem to close in on me. With the frothy Indus gushing powerfully in its suddenly confining channel through the rocks, the blue green waters make a deafening roar and mask out all thoughts except an awed awareness of the strength of the myriad forces which rule our planet Earth. The jagged peaks of black rock have been cut into by the narrow tar road, which seems to flaunt the determination of man who has dared build a road where no roads were meant to be. And soon, as if to prove that nature can wipe out man's puny transgressions at any time it chooses to, a patch of the road ahead has been washed away and the going becomes difficult even for a motorcycle.

A convoy of army trucks is stuck on the other side. I crawl through a rumble of boulders, some of them the size of footballs. This is a tricky manoeuvre but not a dangerous one. I'm at the bottom of a valley and there are no steep cliffs from which to fall off, as was the case near Khardung La. Several people are around and help would certainly be available if I crashed the bike. But I could still break a bone or two if I was too flippant about this, so I slow down to 5 kilometres per hour and get through this mess. My eyes on the rough road, the tight neck strap holding the helmet in place and gloved hands occupied with matters of balance, I feel the presence of something alien in my mouth. That was strange. What in heavens could it be? It is too hard to bite, like a pebble. Fantasy takes flight and I encourage it to believe that a miracle had happened. Could it… Oh. Could it possibly be a divine diamond that the Lords of Lamayuru have bestowed on me? Perhaps those monks were right after all? In the next few minutes, I hazard a guess at its value, and decide on a healthy figure of 15 million US dollars.

Quickly, I get the auction over and the money deposited in my numbered Swiss bank account. And then comes the fun part. Spending it! What would I buy? I've always wanted my own Lear jet and maybe even a yacht. I've also always wanted to start a shelter for orphans and abandoned children I keep seeing on the platforms of India's railway stations. Maybe I'll take a hundred of them on a cruise around the world in my yacht whose size and capacity I mentally increase to required dimensions. Soon the road improves and I can stop.

Bike on its stand, gloves off first, then the helmet and goggles, I rein back my anticipation and pray 'Lord Lamayuru, make it a big diamond… please.' I even promise to call it the Lamayuru Diamond. Carefully, hopefully, I spit out my celestial inheritance on to the palm of my freezing naked hand. I force a stiletto of feigned disappointment into my heart and then the parody falls apart. I am laughing with myself. Oh... ho… ha… ha… it is my wisdom tooth which, aided by the extremely rough road, has finally broken free of its roots and been caught in the enclosed cavity of my mouth. I am amazed at how painless this extraction was. I look at my dislodged tooth with gratitude for half a century of excellent service. It has been a part of this body for five decades and now it is leaving. How many places it had been to. How many types of food it had chewed through. And how many words had flown past it. My fingers caress it for the last time and gently toss it into the Indus. Like the waters of the gurgling river, my tooth might soon find itself in the land of my ancestors. Sindh.

Goodbye dear tooth.

I hope you don't get arrested for blasphemy.

Military trucks plying in long convoys, slow me down considerably and it is already early evening when I park the bike next to the same river Indus flowing through the heart of small-town Kargil, near where the 1999 war was fought. The place bears a fortified look. I ride through the main bazaar and get caught in the evening rush-hour traffic that includes a collection of trucks, cars, scooters, donkey and horse-driven carts, and even one of the double-humped camels of Hunder. Small shops line the narrow road. I am hungry and tired but it is essential that I ride on and get to Dras, which is still 56 kilometres away.

Two voices call out my name and I glance around to see the smiling faces of Irfan, Farzana and Trevor who have just about finished their wayside snack of *samosas* and tea and are also getting ready to take off towards Dras.

It's like meeting long lost loved ones. Not much time to stop and chat though. There'll be time enough for talk later. We all want to get to Dras before nightfall. There is a reason for this haste. The next day's journey will take us through the narrow, treacherous Zoji La, which allows for only one-way traffic that opens up towards Srinagar at 5 a.m. Since it is the gateway from Ladakh into the strife-ridden Kashmir valley, the army checks every vehicle crossing through this pass. That takes time. If we had stayed in Kargil, we would have had to get going at 3 a.m. and ride in the cold and the dark – something that I have avoided after that harrowing ride to Jaipur. This road would sure have spelt suicide that early in the morning.

A convoy of yellow Indian Oil tankers blocks our way. The narrow road allows me no room to overtake them and the next 20 kilometres are slow and smoky, as I crawl on behind them, breathing dust and diesel. Eventually, the truckers let me pass, but the road being rocks and slushy mud, it is still slow going all the way to Dras. The Line of Control (LoC) is not too far away from here. A plaque by the roadside warns, 'The enemy is watching' Already, there is an undercurrent of tension in the air. But the months-long ceasefire is holding and the border which runs parallel to my right, feels safe enough today.

I am now entering the Muslim belt. It is also the first patch of fertile land since I left Nubra valley.

The Indus, which has been flowing through the rocky desert terrain of Ladakh, now has some soil to feed and the results are all around. Large patches of cultivated land add the long-missing dark green to the rust and gold. The green around me soothes the eyes but not the mind. There is an emerging feeling of uneasiness ticking away inside me. I wonder why that is so.

The government tourist lodge is located on the western edge of the Dras valley, right under Tiger Hill. This is where the short war was fought a couple of years ago. It is also the second coldest place on earth. The temperature had dipped to minus 60 degrees Celsius some years ago – a feather in its cap.

But it is Tiger Hill that dominates the ambience here. I turn into the grounds of the government tourist bungalow. Irfan, Farzana and Trevor also arrive at about the same time.

Police presence is all around. After the gruelling 260-kilometre ride from Leh, I am drained to the bone and only thinking of a hot bath, some food and sleep. Wake-up time tomorrow is still 4 a.m. and I'm hoping to get at least six hours of slumber. A tall lanky man approaches. He is the guesthouse keeper, eager to please and obviously desperate to talk with us. He tells us that only two rooms are available and assures us that he will allot them to us. He will also cook us dinner. But only after the *burra sahib* leaves. Their chief officer is on an inspection tour and is expected at the guesthouse any moment.

So the four of us sit on sofas in the porch and wait, not for the 'big guy's' arrival, but rather for his quick and uneventful departure.

The housekeeper, whose name is Abdul Gani, serves us some very good tea and I hungrily munch on glucose biscuits while my three friends quietly digest the *samosas* they ate in Kargil.

Within a few minutes, a white Ambassador with a revolving red pilot light pulls in through the patrolled gate and its arrival jerks everyone around into alertness. I am almost impelled to get up and stand to attention myself. The driver gets out and opens the rear doors. Conditioned as I have been to images of senior police officers who have hair to dye and paunches to belt up, I am absolutely surprised when out steps a young man about 30 years of age, dressed in a white shirt and faded blue jeans. He has an arrogant, jaunty air about him. His first act is to light a cigarette. His junior officers, all older than him by two decades, appear anxious for the inspection to be over with. Dressed in green silk, the police chief's pretty wife alights from the other door and both walk to the room at the very end of the corridor of the guesthouse which has been readied to serve them refreshments. They must be a newly married couple I guess by his eager-to-impress body language while she pretends to look awed but is actually bored.

I was looking forward to some conversation with the police chief and his young wife. Perhaps he would invite us for a drink followed by some nice food. But he looks right through us as he walks to the tea room. Fifteen long minutes later, the entourage snaps to attention a second time. The 'boy chief' lights another cigarette and within 30 seconds everyone is gone. And peace reigns again. It is as if they had never happened.

Abdul Gani, now visibly relaxed, perches on the wooden railing of the porch and when Farzana asks him about Tiger Hill which looms in front of us, re-launches his 'Kargil war' story. I can see he has performed before other audiences and his narration is full of drama and suspense. It's still the top tale in town and this man is a born actor. 'Sahib, it was the shepherd boy who saw them first. He saw the Pakistani soldiers creeping up Tiger Hill and ran back to report this to the Indian Army Captain.'

I cannot completely believe his version of events but I don't want to fuel further conversation. It's a bath I yearn for. The shoulder muscles are knotted up and my arms are sore.

'Hey, Abdul, can I get a bucket of hot water?' I interrupt him.

'Fifteen rupees,' he replies as if in a reflex reaction.

'Ten.'

'Fifteen, but water very hot.'

'All right, Abdul, I'll give you fifteen but I'd like to have it now.'

'Jee haan...', He says and returns to his story. 'We have a spent shell they fired. It's three feet long and exploded right here,' he points to a depression in the foreground. 'Destroyed this whole guesthouse.'

'Abdul... Can I have the hot water please?''Sure... *Haan...Haaan...Abhi laaya*.' The guy can't stop talking even as I spur him on to the kitchen where the wood fires are burning. It's getting colder by the minute. The sun has already dipped beyond the hills.

The water, when it arrives, is scalding hot and I bless Abdul Gani as each mug full of the hot aqua spreads warmth through my knotted muscles. Feeling refreshed and clean, I am better able to give his Kargil war story the attention it deserves.

But we all want food and move to the kitchen, which is warm with the fires blazing within it. There Abdul and another man, who is cooking, talk on as dinner is served. Unbelievably, it's still *dal*-rice on the menu! Abdul Gani drones on till my eyes can no longer stay open. The moon is yet to rise and it is pitch dark as the four of us walk the short distance towards our rooms. Overhead, the night sky is studded with sapphires. I could just reach out and grab a fistful. But the cold will not let me linger outdoors for too long. Trevor and I walk into our room and prepare to rest.

The quilts on the two beds look invitingly warm. It is cold enough to sleep in my riding clothes including socks and jacket. I set the alarm for 4 a.m.

Vroom…Vroom… Four Enfields cruise into the driveway shattering the silence along with any hope of sleep. It could only be….. and it is. Subash, Mani, Varun, Prem and another young guy have been riding in the dark for four hours and have made it to Dras. I had last seen them near Manali ten days ago.

I am quite bushed and was just about to go to sleep but now that will have to be postponed. These guys are hungry and tired – the road from Kargil to Dras is difficult enough even in daylight. The sound of their arrival has got Abdul out of the warm kitchen. He tells them food they can still get from a *dhaba* nearby, but there are no rooms available. There's no alternative but for Trevor to move in with Irfan and Farzana next door. I now have five room mates who crowd into the room, dump their luggage and rush out to find some food. Abdul has told them to hurry before the *dhaba* closes.

When they come back around 10 p.m., everyone is in a mood to talk and recall their day's ride. There is no electricity but I have the Magnalite torch which in candle mode provides subdued light over the room floor full with backpacks and helmets and unfurled sleeping bags. When we finally fall asleep, it is already tomorrow. Wakeup time is in two hours.

Across the Zoji La

It appears I have only just shut my eyes but the mobile alarm insists it was 4 a.m. Brrrr… Don't want to get out of my warm sleeping bag but have to. 'Good morning', I shout to the other sleeping bags. I hate doing this. Waking up everyone like a warden. Reluctantly, they begin to stir. It is almost 5:30 a.m. by the time everyone's bike is loaded and ready to leave. Irfan, Farzana and Trevor have already left at 5 o'clock. I am again part of the group who've told me last night of the numerous breakdowns they've had with each one of their bikes. Subash and Mani's rented 500 cc Enfield broke down near Keylong and that is why they had not met me in Darcha. Varun's motorcycle had overheated the next day and he had had to ride at slow speeds and take frequent halts. Now, as we are just about to kick-start our bikes, it is discovered that Prem's has a flat rear tyre. This means further delay. He decides to inflate the tube and check how big the puncture was. A foot pump is brought out and the tyre inflates and holds. It is only a tiny leak.

Prem wheels out the loaded bike and half rides, half pushes it to the puncture repair shop which our friend Abdul has told us is a kilometre away. I ride on ahead through some rough wet boulder-strewn patches of the road which soon begins to climb towards the Zoji La.

Along the base, I come upon the military checkpoint which is a collection of corrugated tin sheds spread over a broad flat area. Soldiers are everywhere – walking around their olive green trucks which are parked in orderly rows on one side. I have to wait only for 15 minutes before a uniformed, white-haired man comes to tell me I could proceed ahead. No one has checked my bags or my papers.

Is it my honest face or are they just being lax?

The tar and mud road narrows in places allowing for only one-way traffic. Water trickles over shiny black rocky walls where the road has been cut. The temperature is close to zero Celsius. But I am well protected in my high altitude jacket and heavy gloves. The visor keeps the chilling wind from freezing my face and the balaclava under my helmet keeps my head warm. After an hour of steady climbing on this wet rocky road, I arrive on the top of the pass – the Zoji La (3,529 metres).

This pass is not as high as some of the others I had crossed but it is the coldest. Crowded around by peaks, which on the Ladakh side are naked brown with no greenery and on the Kashmir valley side lush with pine, this is a spectacular place. A thick mantle of snow covers all peaks even this early in July. If this is summer, what must winter be?

Sanjay, the fifth guy who had come in with the others last night, has been riding behind me and soon joins me. We smoke cigarettes and take pictures of each other. We didn't get a chance to talk much last night. He's from Delhi – a student of architecture. After a few minutes, he rides off. I want to spend some more minutes on this last stretch of Ladakh.

It is a moment of goodbye. Tranquil Ladakh, the northernmost corner of my vast country. Frontier land. So unique. Unforgiving terrain with forgiving people. The air of the land sweetened with the compassion of Buddha. The quiet dignified stark honesty on smiling faces. Timelessness etched on the monasteries. And silences like I've never heard before. Here the wind is a palpable presence. It talks to you in cosmic whispers. The mountains of the Himalayas, although physically foreboding, seem to exude something other than just awe. All through my journey in Ladakh, I have felt safe amidst these giants of rock and ice. But this is soon to change. This is my last moment of peace. On the other side is the tumultuous vale of Kashmir.

A shallow road-river bisects the way ahead. It is two feet deep at its midpoint. My brain is too numb to order my feet to stop. I feel like a spectator as I sense my forearms firm up, hands tighten their grip on the handle and without pause the bike plunges into the chilly water and is out on the other side before I have time to be afraid. I did feel the wheels slip over the smooth boulders and had almost lost balance as the bike was coming up over the last edge of washed-away road before the ground firmed up. But I am across the obstacle and ready to begin my descent into the green Kashmir valley.

Coming down the pass is a much tougher task as the narrow one-way road is packed bumper to bumper by a military convoy. One of the trucks has a problem and everyone behind it is stuck. Not even enough space for a motorcycle to edge through. Everyone has switched off their engines which means this might be a long wait. An hour later the convoy begins to crawl ahead but within minutes there is a loud sharp noise which sounds like someone has fired a shot but is actually a tyre burst in a huge Stallion truck just ahead of me. Again the convoy grinds to a halt. Soldiers jump out of the stricken truck and immediately get to work, replacing the punctured tyre. But this time I'm able to sneak through the three feet of clearance between the truck and the cliff wall and am on my way out of the block hole.

It still is slow going because of the rest of the crawling convoy. In any case, it is impossible to go any faster than the ten kilometres per hour I'm clocking. Fallen rocks have been swept away and piled in heaps on the side, further narrowing the passage. But if trucks can go, so can a motorcycle and after only 30 minutes, the road suddenly turns character and becomes a smooth two-lane highway maintained in immaculate condition by the hardy folk of the BRO.

I am through the Zoji La and have entered Kashmir.

The Valley of Tears

I stop on a broad patch of road that is firm enough for the bike to stand on. An army *jawan* in a bullet-proof jacket, his head also protected by bullet-proof covering, stands guard with a gun clasped in both hands and its muzzle pointing to the ground. I can see he's on alert as he watches me take my own headgear off. He relaxes once he sees my white hair. There are some advantages to being old. We walk up to each other and exchange greetings. The morning air has an invigorating nip to it. Our breath comes out as if we were smoking. I pull out my water bottle and drink up half a litre of its contents. He stands quietly as I take out my cigarette packet. When I offer him one, he accepts and smokes it with obvious relish. He says he's from a village near Rae Bareily. He's spent three years in Pune, which was a choice family posting and a very enjoyable period for him. We chat about Pune for a few minutes. I'm in no hurry to move. Standing in the morning sunlight is a good way to warm my chilled body. I sit on a milestone and finish my cigarette.

An old bearded man in Kashmiri dress and wearing a fez cap is climbing towards us from the Sonamarg side. He is leading a donkey which has empty gunnysacks hanging limply on either side over its back. Both man and animal are walking with heads bent, eyes watching their feet. The soldier crosses the road towards the old man and stops him. *'Kya hai inme?'* (What's in these?) He asks curtly as he checks the sacks. Finding nothing, he stands back before nodding to tell the man he can go. The old man walks away without a word, holding on to the rope as the donkey leads the way. I wonder what the donkey thinks of this exchange between these two bipeds.

Back at his post again, the soldier tells me that it is the time of the annual Amarnath *yatra* and the army is expecting militants to target this Hindu pilgrimage, as they do each year. Scores of people have been killed in attacks but thousands more keep coming. This year the army has made especially stringent arrangements and security has been beefed up to an unprecedented level.

When I roll into Sonamarg, I see a large number of eateries shack-hotels set up to cater to tourists. I stop at one, gratefully sink into a plastic chair outside and ask for a double-egg omelette and two butter *parathas*...

The waiter-cum-cook says it will take 20 minutes to get them ready so I request a cup tea first.

Across the road is a stretch of flat grassland where over 20 SUVs are parked in a row, waiting for tourists. Behind this melee rises a green pineclothed mountain. A number of ponies led by tall, strong-looking men, who are coolies, wait for loads to pick. As I sip my tea, a covered half-ton truck packed with folded aluminium chairs, beds and mattresses is stopped at the military checkpoint towards my left. A *jawan* gestures for the driver and his companion to get down and let him inspect the truck. On seeing the cargo, he asks the driver to unload it. This angers the driver who yells that he cannot unload everything. It took him four hours to load the truck. Soon a crowd of locals collects and starts shouting slogans against the army. This brings a senior officer out of his cabin and he tries to reason with the crowd which is only getting more boisterous and vocal. This could turn into a full-fledged riot quite easily and I am worried my motorcycle, with its Maharashtra number, might become the target of the enraged mob. I cancel my breakfast order and leave a five-rupee coin to pay for my tea. Donning my helmet, I quickly kick-start the motorcycle and leave the scene. I am now only a 100 kilometres away from Srinagar. All along the route, every 100 metres, I see an armed sentry keeping watch over vehicles that ply this route, carting pilgrims to the Amarnath caves. The road is nice enough and the setting is picture postcard perfect. The ingredients are all there. High mountains on either side, crowded with pine and crowned with snow which blazes white in the morning sun. The Indus – gushing strongly on the left along the road. A cool breeze is blowing gently. But I am not at ease. The strong army presence just cannot be ignored away. The tension between them and the local people is palpable.

Ahead of me, a convoy of dark green Stallion trucks full of armed soldiers comes to a halt and I do the same. Each truck has a machine gun mounted in front with a soldier with his finger on the trigger. These men all wear black bandannas which cover their heads and faces, leaving only a slit open for the eyes. They look intimidating. I keep my helmet with its dark visor on and stare at the faces of the *jawans* sitting shoulder to shoulder inside the truck just ahead of me. They all seem to be middle-aged men, some with potbellies and all with grim faces. Frontline soldiers for whom the possibility of being blown up or shot looms as a frightening reality every day.

A huge explosion suddenly rips the silence apart. This time however, it is not a militant attack but dynamite which is being used to blast the rocky mountain and broaden this road. I take off my helmet and the *jawans*, who have been staring at me all this while, can now see my face. I nod and smile at them and they wave back. Two of them smile. After about half an hour, the 'go' signal is given and the convoy is on the move.

I am now desperate for food. I stop at a small shop where I hope to get some breakfast but all they have is tea and biscuits. As I sit around waiting for the tea to be made, I am surrounded by four young boys each holding a plastic bag full of small green apples. 10 rupees only. I take one bag but the fruit has been picked too early and is too unripe to eat even in my state of starvation. The tea stall owner is a tall, old man with a flowing white beard. His two grown sons also come around to sit near me and I try to strike a conversation. Their reaction is initially quite guarded, not at all friendly – they don't seem to like 'Indians' here. When I tell them about myself and my work, the old man then says something to his sons and one of them walks away into the back of the shop. I can't understand a bit of their language and wonder what this is all about. In a few minutes, the son returns pulling a 5 year old boy. The child looks at me with frightened eyes and begins to cry. I smile and make a gentle gesture towards him but the boy doesn't come near me and clings to his grandfather.

The old man says that his grandson cannot yet speak and since I'm a speech doctor, maybe I can help him? I examine the child's tongue – looks normal. Then I conduct a crude hearing test and realize he must suffer from severe sensori-neural hearing loss, beyond reaping the benefit of even the most powerful of hearing aids. Ideally, this child should be in a school for the hearing impaired, but not only are there no such schools here, the family does not look as if they can afford any special education for him. I explain that the child's hearing problem cannot be helped through any 'operation'. This advice does not do anything to make me popular with this poor Kashmiri family. I've only increased their feelings of helplessness. The child runs away from me and silence descends on us all.

I've already devoured a pack of glucose biscuits and drunk two cups of tea and it is time to go anyway.

With still two hours of daylight left, I ride into Srinagar.

Decades ago, when Kashmir was free of militancy, it had been a different story. Streets crowded with travellers from every country in the world. A paradise for young backpackers.

Today this is all changed. The security drills of the army and the police, the check posts, the frisking of the citizenry, everything contributes to creating a hostile ambience. There is no joy to be had around here.

A few locals and Indian tourists walk on the streets but it is the army and police personnel who dominate the scene. I decide against living on a houseboat because then, I'd have to leave my motorcycle parked in an open parking lot and I really don't want to do that. I ride through the gate of what looks like a hotel. This building I'm entering might offer good food and lodging. All I'm dreaming about is mutton *biryani.* An army sentry with an automatic rifle stops me and says I cannot enter because this building is commandeered by the military and no rooms are available for civilians.

As I exit through the other gate, I am stopped by a thin, *salwaar-kameez*-clad man who says he can find me a place to stay. His name, he tells me in a tone suggesting great regard for himself, is Salama, tourist guide. He is about 40 years old and has a hungry, malnourished look. He seems desperate for my patronage. Money must be hard to come by in tourist-starved Kashmir. Everything around here looks sombre. As if in mourning for the lost days of prosperity and happiness. This year has promised to be better, with more Indian tourists venturing into the valley for recreational or religious reasons.

I am hungry and exhausted and don't have much will to get into any kind of prolonged conversation but Salama drones on and on about this very lovely and cheap houseboat, which he says would be ideal for me. I have taken an instant dislike to him but have no energy to resist his insistent sales chatter. He half forces me to park my motorcycle in the public parking lot and then helps me cart my saddle-bags to the shore of the Dal Lake where he hires a *shikara* to take me behind the first few rows of the five-star houseboats into the murky inner waters of the still lake. This is the non-glamorous part, where the locals live. A faint stink pervades the area around and not surprisingly, since I spot a few pieces of excreta bobbing in the waters along with a myriad other rotting debris. I really wouldn't like to stay anywhere near here.

'*Janaab, yeh kahaan leke ja rahe ho*?' (Where are you taking me?) I ask him.

'Aarrey Sahib, you just see for one time. You like my houseboat,' he replies and now I realize that he is taking me to his own houseboat. My protests are to no avail and, captive as I am in the *shikara,* I have no choice but to wait till it docks with a houseboat moored amongst many others. This one is not very well maintained from the outside, with much of the paint peeled away. I follow Salama into the central room which opens into the kitchen on my left and into what I presume must be the guestroom he wants me to take on the right.

A fair, good-looking woman of about 40, dressed in a *salwaar-kameez* made of satin and with her head and face covered with her *dupatta,* comes out of the kitchen and Salama tells me she's his wife. He then entreats me to take off my shoes and come see the guestroom. Reluctantly I oblige him. Even unlacing the shoes and pulling them off my feet is a demanding task. The heavily carpeted room, its walls covered with thick, pink-coloured curtains and with most of its floor space occupied by the central bed is already making me feel claustrophobic. When he tells me that the toilet is across the boat through the kitchen and his own bedroom, I decide enough was enough. In a curt tone, I say I don't want his room and could he please take me back to the houseboats in the front row facing the lake road.

Half an hour later and for 500 rupees, I get myself a room on a large well kept houseboat which has ten more rooms, all of them vacant. I am the only guest.

Now I am really hungry and want to go looking for a good restaurant where I could get my much fantasized about mutton *biryani*. In my present state of fatigue, I would rather have it brought to me. Salama, who is still hovering nearby, again offers his services. I give him a 100-rupee note but he demands 50 more. I ask him to bring me lots of good *biryani* and fast. As his *shikara* vanishes into the darkening waters, I lie down and wait. Only 20 minutes later, Salama is back. He has brought my 'lovely'*biryani* in a plastic wrapper, dripping oil. When I pour it out on a plate, my heart sinks. The *biryani* has one small piece of mutton hiding in a cupful of rice and drowning in oil. I yell at Salama:

'Yeh kya laye ho?' (What is this you've brought?) He says it is very good *biryani* and he has taken a lot of trouble getting it for me. He then tells me he's paid 150 rupees for it. I lose my cool and ask him to get out. After he leaves, I try eating my 'very good *biryani*' but can't. It is so heavily spiced and has been cooked in so much oil that even in my ravenously hungry condition, I am nauseated by its sight and smell and have to open the window and dump the mess into the lake.

There is no service available on this houseboat. No one comes to ask if I need anything. I am starving, tired to the bone and mentally frazzled. I've pushed myself to the limit. Two days have passed since I left Leh. The terrain, the lack of food and sleep and now the tense situation around me are taking their toll. I smoke a cigarette to kill my hunger and stare out of the single window which has in view other houseboats, their dimmed lights reflected in the dark waters.

My mind is an absolute blank but it is not the conscious 'no thought' state of a meditator. My last thought is a prayer for the safety of my motorcycle, my only buddy in town, parked alone in the cold, on the road bordering placid lake.

Halfway through the night, I wake up to the sound of a growling cat only to realize that the walls of my empty stomach are contracting in protest. I could easily slip into a state of delirium.

Shall I let myself go?

My own experiences with delirium have been so rare that I want to really enjoy this precious state of awareness for the short time that such moments normally last. I know that I'll get food tomorrow and assure myself that my condition is not serious.

I let my mind travel free – go where it will.

A state of delirium frees the mind and body from its strongly conditioned dependence on the five senses which monitor its own place in time and space. In this 'conscious delirium', I shrug off the force of gravity that normally keeps me rooted to earth. I soar off out of the window and over the darkened lake. Like a trapeze artist, I land briefly on the road and then push off with a bend of my knees to propel myself over buildings and farms and then, as I get more adventurous, I am flying over the icy Himalayas – miles and miles of them. I count peaks instead of sheep and slide back into sleep.

I wake up early and pack my bags. The lake seems to be emerging from its dark mantle. A kingfisher plops into the water and comes up with a tiny fish in its beak. It flies off only to return for an encore. At least someone is getting breakfast. A *shikara* full of flowers is approaching me. An old man with a white flowing beard rows it to under my window and tries to sell me some. I tell him I can't buy any flowers. I'm on a bike. In that case, he says, he can sell me some seeds. He has them ready in an envelope and we settle on the price. Eighty rupees for eight varieties of flowers. Chrysanthemums, dahlias, zinnias. I ask if he can get me a *shikara*. It comes after an hour-long wait.

I reach the road and walk awkwardly with my luggage towards the parking lot, anxious to see my motorcycle. A sigh of relief! It stands where I had left it. The parking lot is also where private tourist vehicles ply from, and this being the Amarnath yatra season, there are many drivers warming up the engines of their SUVs. I strap the saddle-bags on to the bike and then walk up to a nearby tea stall and drink the thickest, sweetest glass of tea I've ever had. To my stomach, which is by now resigned to its state of starvation, the tea is food. Feels so good, I ask for a second round.

Fortified to an extent by this liquid breakfast, I walk back to the bike and do a maintenance check. Taking me over the Zoji La, the engine has used up a lot of oil, so I top up the deficit and then I'm ready to leave this stricken valley.

I am out of Srinagar and moving towards Anantnag. National Highway 1A from Srinagar to Jammu is in very good condition with not one pothole in sight. Armed, bulletproofed sentries dot it like milestones every 500 metres. The tea I've drunk now wants out. I need to pee but every time I slow down to stop, a nearby sentry signals me to move on. No stopping. Finally, I can wait no longer and have to choose between wetting my pants and getting shot. I stop and get off the bike. A sentry approaches me cautiously with his gun cocked and ready. As far as he knows, I could well be carrying explosives in my stuffed bags. Without making any sudden moves, I slowly move my hands upwards and remove my helmet. He relaxes when he sees my white hair. I walk over to water the nearby deodar and then get talking with the soldier. He is a young man from somewhere in Bihar and hates his current posting. Raunaq Lal, standing there alone amidst a hostile local population, is bursting with a need to talk with someone whose national loyalty he could trust. Like everyone else, he is waiting for his annual leave. Anxious to get out of this vale of death, where every minute, there was the possibility of being blown up into smithereens. He's seen it happen often enough. Only two days ago, a truck had been targeted on this very road, he tells me. Twenty-two soldiers had died.

He had some hot tea in a thermos and eagerly offers me some. While I sip the welcome brew from his army-issue mug, Raunaq Lal tells me how they conduct security operations in the nearby villages, which he says are a hot bed of militancy. They surround a suspected militant hideout; there is an exchange of automatic fire claiming casualties on all sides.

'Koi bhi maara ja sakta hai,' (Anyone can get killed) he says. Many such raids inevitably result in some civilian casualties, which further alienate the Kashmiri people from mainstream India. I cry for Kashmir in my heart. Who has put a curse on this lovely valley? And how are we ever going to get out of this?

As I get up to go, an olive green army truck stops and Raunaq runs to it to collect his lunch. It comes in a tiffin carrier with four large compartments full with, I am sure, very good food. My new friend tells me he will eat his lunch at noon with another soldier standing guard near him.

'Khaana khaate samay kuchh bhi ho sakta hai.' (Anything can happen while we eat our lunch.)

These guys live from minute to minute.

I say my goodbye and as I restart the bike, I feel guilty about heading home while young Raunaq yearns for his.

A *dhaba* with a pot bubbling, with what I hope is mutton curry, is where I stop next. When I ask what's available, the answer still is the inevitable *dal* and rice. But I'm too hungry to complain. I gulp down my food and top it up with tea before riding on towards Anantnag. With a full stomach, the world suddenly seems a better place. I feel good to be riding on a road that will take me out of the high mountains surrounding the Kashmir valley.

Most of the traffic is military. There are olive green buses carting soldiers between Srinagar and Jammu. The happier looking ones are headed out of the valley, many on their much dreamed about annual leave.

Ahead of me, as the road turns around a hillock on my left, I see a group of around ten young men rushing down towards me frantically waving their hands, signalling me to stop. Most of them are in T-shirts and three or four have fuzz around their faces, which, with their dry uncut hair, makes them look like desperados. Two of them reach the edge of the tar road before I do and stand in my way. This could be the dangerous situation which has eluded me all this while. Perhaps these are militants who will either kidnap me or shoot me right there. After all, I'm passing through an area known for such attacks. I consider dodging them and speeding away but in an instant it is too late and I can do nothing but stop. Mixed feelings of fear and thrill. Finally, some excitement. I don't know how this scenario will unfold.

As I remove my helmet the desperados surround me and then one asks if I am from Maharashtra. I wonder if this is some kind of a test question but the mystery is solved when he tells me they are all soldiers from the Maratha Regiment and when they had spotted my bike's MH licence number, they had rushed down from their barracks to meet someone from their home state. They too are homesick and probably see me as their connection with their beloved hometowns. They insist I visit their barracks. I tell them that I need to reach Jammu that evening and it is already mid-afternoon, but they will not let me go. Enthusiastically, like excited children, they take me to their camp overlooking a deep chasm of the valley, not far from the highway. There are two rooms erected from prefabricated fibreglass. Long cylinders cut lengthwise and placed in parallel. Inside the one I enter are 14 beds with cupboards and tiny tables beside each. Every available wall space is crowded with posters of Aishwarya Rai and Rani Mukherjee who appeared to be the current favourites. In one corner, Rekha in her Umrao Jaan attire is sitting in the midst of a *mujra*.

Next to the door, on my left and mounted on a high shelf are a television set and a DVD player. Tanuja is enticing a harassed Dev Anand with '*Raat akeli hai*' but no one is watching. They must have seen this number before. Someone places a huge stainless steel glass of *lassi* in my hand. The boys want to listen to me talking in Marathi. The unshaven one dressed in black T-shirt and jeans, who had stopped me on the road, says his name is Shivnath and he is from Akurdi which is about 25 kilometres from where I live in Pune. He wants me to phone his home and tell his mother and sister that he was fine. That was a brave message because I can see that none of them is 'fine'. The moment-to-moment stress is taking its toll. They try to camouflage it by an outward show of bravado but these young men, so far away from their homes, standing around me, look like lonely children marooned in a dangerous world. Dilawar, a Sikh boy/man from Nanded who speaks Marathi like a native, clicks a picture of the group. We all look like outlaws in it.

When I get up to leave, I realize I am weighed down with the unfamiliar feeling of guilt. It feels as if I am abandoning them to their fate. How many of these soldiers will survive the year in this hostile climate? Will I, sitting comfortably in my chair at home a week from now, sipping my coffee, read about an ambush or an explosion which had snatched away these lives? Will Shivnath get married and have a family? Or are his mother and sister destined to get that dreaded message which will tell them he was gone?

These morbid thoughts do nothing to lift my spirits. I force a smile as I wish them goodbye. Only when I am back on the road with my face hidden under the helmet do I let my laden dam overflow. I am crying. I feel an empty void in my stomach. For the first time I have understood the soldier's sacrifice for his country. Paying with his life for those who use nationalism or religion to keep the broth of human misery boiling.

A Most Dangerous Man

A board on my left announces that this is my last view of the Kashmir valley. I am not too unhappy about that – anxious in fact to leave it.

At Banihal, a high mountain rises, sitting right in the middle of the road. I am at the mouth of the Jawahar Tunnel. I have to pass through a security check conducted by the J&K police. The check post has the air of a picnic spot. While three Sumos wait in line for clearance, their occupants have spilled out and are busy providing patronage to a nearby tea stall. They are returning from their Amarnath yatra. After the two days I've now spent in the sombre and tense atmosphere of Sonamarg and Srinagar, the bawdy demeanour of some of the youth and the loud *'Jai Mata-di'* songs blaring from their vehicles, which normally would make me cringe, today seem to signal my return to the happy, if noisy chaos of an India I am comfortable with, at least right now.

Like the previous one at Dras, this check is also quite cursory and I am allowed to proceed. Tunnels are my least favourite places to ride through. This is a long one. The dark rocky walls of this dimly lit tunnel close in on me, like a cave, and I feel claustrophobic. I pull up the visor for better visibility. There are patches of oil that could cause the bike to slip and my speed is a slow ten kilometres per hour. After an interminable 20 minutes, I sight the light at the end of the tunnel. In another moment, I'm out of it.

I have a ticket on the Jammu-Tawi Express which will take me and my motorcycle to Pune but I still have a day to spare and decide to spend the night at Patnitop (2,024 metres). Just off the highway, this resort town has many hotels tucked away amongst dense deodar forests. I stop at a *chai* shop near the bus stop where a few travellers stand or walk around. One group is on its way to Amarnath.

A fair young man of smallish build approaches me and hands me a visiting card.

Hotel Gulmohar.

'Room Sir?'

'*Haan. Kahan hai*?' (Yes, where is it?)

He says he can take me there and I realize he means he will ride pillion. My luggage has encroached on the rear seat and there is very little space but he doesn't even mention this and perched perilously on the saddle-bags, guides me towards the hotel. The road is narrow, steep and unpaved and in my weakened condition, I have to be careful I don't crash the bike. The last bit of the road is precipitous and I ask him to dismount and then make it to the top in first gear. But one look around and I know the effort has been worth it. Hotel Gulmohur is indeed lovely. Built with deodar logs, the small hotel has two suites. Mine is a two room affair with the front room furnished with a cosy sofa set with a centre table to rest one's legs on. Inside is the bedroom with a queen size bed covered with quilts. An electric heater stands in the corner, ready to heat the room. The spicy aroma of chicken curry floats in from under the closed door. The kitchen is on the other side of the bedroom wall. Tantalized, my gastric juices are all ready for the upcoming action. Finally I'm going to eat real food. I have no energy to undress or take a bath. My hip flask still holds a peg of rum. I drain the last drops into a glass and sit on the sofa to sip it as I wait for nirvana.

Finally a waiter brings in the dinner and unveils the covered plates. I almost have an orgasm! The curry looks absolutely fabulous. I say a quick pre-dinner thanks to the chicken and plunge into my royal meal. The waiter keeps the supply of hot *rotis* coming. As the enriching food slips down my gullet,

I can actually feel the cells of my body begin to come alive. Parched earth being watered. Ten *rotis* later I am satiated.

Sleep comes easy on a full stomach.

I am awakened by the sound of quarrelling magpies. As I crawl out of bed and open the door, the aroma of deodar fills my lungs. Wish I could take this fragrance home. I pick up a few fallen twigs. The mountainside is splattered with patches of iced snow. It is chilly here and I have to zip up my jacket to stop a shiver.

Jammu is not too far away and I can afford to take it a bit easy today. Last night's dinner has rejuvenated my body. A feeling of well-being vibrates through me. The morning air is deliciously fresh and chilly. The magpies flutter in arrow-straight flight, to and from their nests. Other smaller birds twitter in the bushes that are spread around the hotel. These are the very last hours of cold for me. Jammu is going to be in the throes of a sweltering summer.

I won't need my fur lined gloves or my balaclava anymore. My warm boots are just extra baggage now. I empty my bags of all these things, which I hand over to Mukesh (the waiter) who accepts them happily. Now there is room in my saddle-bags for the deodar twigs which join the colourful rocks I had picked in the Nubra Valley at the bottom of the saddle-bag.

I leave Hotel Gulmohar to rejoin the highway and begin my final descent from the mountains.

Within an hour of leaving Patnitop, I am sweating. I stop at a small stall next to a bus stop. Two middle aged men are having tea and seeing my Maharashtra number plates, their curiosity makes them invite me to sit on the vacant chair at their table. One of them is overweight for his five-and-a-half feet frame while the other one is fitter and looks smart with his Chaplinesque mustache. They tell me they both work for the Jammu Water Works and are waiting for a bus to take them there. They are on the 4 p.m. to midnight shift.

Once I've answered their questions by telling them my name, place of origin, my profession, my parentage, how many children I have and how much money I earn, the plump man asks if I am planning to visit the Vaishnodevi temple. I tell them that I've a train to catch that night. This information does not make Chaplin happy at all.

'Vaishnodevi you must see!' he exclaims a bit too loudly. His companion nods in agreement.

'Durga, Laxmi, Saraswati. All in one. Only temple in the world with all three goddesses in one!' Chaplin says.

I nod and smile and tell them I would like to have

gone there but I'm too worn out to travel any further.

They seem offended. But I am saved from further remarks by the arrival of their bus. Both get up and rush towards the bus. I wave out to them as they find seats. Chaplin then leans out of the window of the bus and yells 'Go by helicopter'. The bus leaves in a cloud of dust. I pay the waiter for my tea and get astride the motorcycle.

I ride through the crowded city asking for directions to the railway station where I have to board the Jammu-Tawi Express. The train will leave at 9:30 p.m. and I have four hours in which to get the motorcycle booked as freight and then get some dinner. The luggage office is a large godown located within the station. A Sikh railway policeman helps me push the motorcycle up the concrete incline. He directs me to read a paper notice pasted along with many others on the wall. The procedure for loading two-wheelers apparently involves completely emptying the petrol tank, taking off the mirrors, getting the bike wrapped in hay and gunnysack, then attaching a metal plate with the recipient's address painted on it. The Sikh policeman tells a bearded man standing nearby to help me get the bike ready for loading which he does with the help of a young boy. The bike is wrapped for its long train ride to Pune. The female clerk at the table then checks ownership and insurance papers, accepts the fees and that's it. By the time the bike is out of my hands it is 7:30 p.m. I still have two hours to stroll around the station and eat dinner.

Jammu railway station is the arrival and departure point for travellers to Vaishnodevi and Amarnath. A large *maidan* across the station has been converted into a brightly lit eating area where over 50 food shacks cater to the travellers, providing them every kind of food – from Jain *thalis* and Punjabi food to Chinese and Italian cuisine.

The sky is now almost completely covered by dark rain clouds. I walk up to a stall that offers Rajasthani food and settle for *poori* and *aloo bhaji* which is served on a folded page of the Jammu edition of The Indian Express. I quickly finish dinner and walk back to stand under the metal roofed outer area of the railway station and watch lightning forking down the sky in spidery streaks followed by clashes of thunder. There is electricity in the air.

As I make my way towards Platform No. 1, I see that the Jammu-Tawi Express has already arrived. I lug my bags towards the second-AC coach.

My co-passengers are three elderly men who are busy arranging their luggage. It strikes me that they are all dressed in identical fashion; each wearing white cotton pyjamas and a thin, short-sleeved shirt.

Almost like a uniform. They are talking to each other in Gujarati. I have been assigned a lower berth and one of them asks me if I could exchange mine with his.

'I have arthritis and cannot climb up,' he informs me in a friendly manner. I've no objection to this. In fact, it is an advantageous exchange for me. The upper berth will allow for undisturbed slumber.

It is already 10 o'clock in the morning when I finally wake up. I descend from my perch and land right in the midst of a conversation. My three fellow travellers are sitting around an open container full of *ganthias*, and one by one, each helps himself to a fistful of the snack. As I sit with them, one of them offers me the *ganthias*, and appears pleased when I take a few.

They are from Jhansi and are disciples of 'Motababa' who, they say, is an enlightened guru with divine powers. They seem anxious to tell me more about their spiritual master but my senses are saturated with the divinity of the Himalayas and all I want to do is to go to my berth and slip back into my somnolent condition.

I've been on the train for two nights and feel

refreshed after my marathon slumber. The white-clad men are gone. Another seven hours and I too will be home.

But I am yet to meet the most dangerous man I encountered on my month-long 4,300 km journey.

At first glance, there is nothing you see that would mark him as unusual. What could be more ordinary than a ticket checker checking tickets? White shirt and trousers, a black cotton coat frayed at the cuffs. His plastic name plate hangs limply from the top of his right coat pocket. R.N. Sharma, it proclaims almost apologetically. He himself looks worn out and harmless. His fringe of white hair suggests he is probably close to retirement. With that in mind, he might have decided against putting money into a new coat or indeed, new shoes. He has a large vermilion mark on his forehead and is wearing a necklace of grape sized *rudraksha*, but even that is not an uncommon sight in religion-obsessed India.

He is carrying the black briefcase typical of his office and after he has finished his rounds he chooses to come and sit on the now vacant seats under my upper berth. I have a clear view of his well-oiled scalp which a diligent comb has tried its best to cover up with the few strands of hair available to it. He has placed his briefcase on the seat and then removed his shoes and now sits with his legs crossed under him. When he opens his briefcase, I can see it is really a portable shrine.

No papers or files occupy the august space within. He has stuffed the passenger lists and his receipt book into the pockets of his coat. Instead, the inside cover of the lid of his briefcase is lined with pictures of numerous deities who seem to vie for place in the limited space available to them. The briefcase itself is full of things used in the ritual of prayer. A tiny brass bell, a few hibiscus flowers, a container full of vermilion powder and wrapped in a handkerchief of thin red nylon is a book which he is now uncovering. It seems to be a much used document – the paper is smudged with fingerprints in various colours. The briefcase also holds an open, clay oil lamp, which the gentleman now proceeds to light. He first takes a tuft of cotton, deftly rolls it into a wick and places it in the *diya*. He then unscrews a small brown bottle and tilts it enough to fill the *diya* with oil. He now takes a matchbox and strikes. He strikes the match but the lighted stick snaps and flies off to hit the thick cloth curtains hanging close by. Fortunately the fire fizzles out before any damage is done. I am beginning to feel uncomfortable. What if the curtains had caught fire? The coach has a sizable quantity of inflammable materials. The seats are foam covered with rexine. Very combustible. Hasn't he read the fire warning notices displayed so prominently in every compartment? Surely part of his responsibilities would be to ensure that passengers observed these rules?

But Shri Sharma doesn't seem deterred by any such considerations. He has struck another match and managed to light the lamp. He has placed the *diya*, now burning with an inch long flame, in the centre of his briefcase next to the cinder-dry book. The plastic bottle of extra oil rolls around nearby. With closed eyes, his hands devoutly folded, he is murmuring what sounds like a prayer.

My eyes are glued to the unsteady lamp. I imagine it tipping over, spilling burning oil on to paper and plastic and the fire spreading rapidly to the curtains and the thin cotton bed sheets and foam filled pillows.

Am I being paranoid? I don't really need any of this. My mind wants to drift off and go sit on that rock near Suraj Tal. But with Sharmaji doing what he is, I am compelled to deal with the situation enacting itself three feet below me. I decide to trust my fears and jump down to land in front of the unperturbed devotee. I take two towels from the heap left by a departed passenger and quickly go to the water basin and wet them under the tap. I then return and sit across the ticket collector, ready to smother any fire that his ritual might start. Maybe it is fatigue that is making me act this way but I just can't seem to relax. My mind is stuck on preventing a possible fire.

I consider making a ruckus and stopping his dangerous devotions.

I think about taking a picture and writing to the railway safety board.

I ruminate upon making it the topic of a newspaper exposé.

But all I do is stay tense and silent. I am in no mood for any kind of confrontation. I tell myself to calm down.

I begin to think kindly thoughts about Sharmaji. Maybe the man is scared of death and is earning some *punya*-points with his gods. He's just doing what he thinks is a very 'good' thing. After all, who can discount the virtues of prayer? That he is completely unaware of his fire-making capabilities is his ignorance not malice. I try and force myself to forgive him and resolve to talk to him about it in a nice, gentle way.

He finally completes his prayer and opens his eyes. He now takes up the bell and tinkles it loudly for a minute, douses the flame with his fingers, folds his book and packs up his briefcase. All his actions are businesslike. He then unfurls his legs, turns around and looks at me with the smug expression of a child who has finished his homework for the day and is expecting to be praised. I remain silent and unencouraging. I've only half succeeded in comforting myself.

He then takes a bar of chocolate from a side pocket of his coat and breaking it in two, hands me the larger part.

'*Prasad*,' he says sheepishly.

I suddenly don't have the heart to be angry with him or lecture him on fire hazards and safety. Instead, I put the wet towels on the small wall table and bite on the chocolate.

Epilogue

Juhi is startled when she sees me get out of the train – my face is a shade of dark chocolate and I now have a scraggly beard. She hesitates before convincing herself that I am indeed the same clean-shaven, plump-faced dad she had said goodbye to a month ago.

I can now see Meena coming towards me followed by an elderly lady who is holding a garland of marigold flowers. As they come closer I recognize Esther D'Costa. She is dressed in a white sari. Her face looks serene and peaceful. She is smiling as she extends her arms and puts the garland around my neck. Suddenly, I feel like a celebrity. She then opens the hand bag she's carrying, takes out a packet and puts it in my hands. It feels heavy. When I ask her what it is, all she does is smile and say that Jeremy would have wanted me to have it.

As we all walk out of the platform, I can see everyone staring at me. The TC does not ask me for my ticket. The garland must make me look like someone important.

I am home, lying on my own bed. The familiarity of the room is reassuring. I've been indulging my body. Oil massages. Hot baths. As much of anything as it desires to eat or drink. And rest, rest, rest.

The mind is free to receive radio broadcasts from wherever it wants. It can wander over to sit with the Sufi Baba, hear the *shabad* in the Kiratpur *gurudwara* or the sound of roaring river Parvati. It can feel the caress of the breeze filtering in through the deodar forest on the road to Manali.

Or remember the smell of Tsering's cow!

Mr. D'Costa's parting gift to me, a slim, flat, steel box with the BMW logo embossed on it, is a toolbox for motorcycles.

Glossary of Hindi Words

'Abhi laaya'	- I'll get it right away
adivasi	- tribal
aloo	- potato
Aswin –Poornima	- October full moon
balcao	- sit out, usual in Goan houses
bakra	- goat, here one who can be fooled
bhelpuriwalas	- hawkers with carts selling snacks
bhikshuk	- a monk who begs for his food
bhujiya	- egg scrambled with onions, coriander and chillies
bidi	- strong cigarette rolled in tobacco leaf
biryani	- mutton or chicken cooked in spiced rice
burra	- big
chai	- tea
channawalla	- hawker selling gram and peanuts
charpai	- wooden framed rope bed
chela	- disciple
chikoos	- tropical fruit

Choli ke peeche kya hai	- 'What's behind the blouse?'- Title of popular ribald Hindi film song.
daaktar	- doctor
dal	- lentil
degchi	- large cooking pot
devi mata	- mother goddess
dhaba	- small road-side eating place
dhoti	- man's garment worn waist downwards
diya	- small clay lamp
dum	- courage / guts
dupatta	- long scarf worn by women
feni	*- Goan drink made from palm or cashew.*
ganthias	- crisp snack
gaon	- village
ghat	- hilly terrain
gompa	- Buddhist shrine
harbara	- green gram
haveli	- large house
holi	- Indian festival of colour
janaab	- polite manner of addressing a man
Jee Sahab	- yes sir
jilebees	- Indian sweet
kadak	- strong
kurta	- knee length shirt
langoor	- free kitchen in Sikh gurudwaras

langar	- black faced, light grey monkey with long tail
lassi	- drink made from yogurt
lungi	- sarong like unstiched garment
maidan	- open ground
majlis	- celebratory party
masala	- spice
mela	- fair
modak ladoos	- favourite sweet of Lord Ganesha.
mojdis	- leather shoes
mujra	- song and dance usually by nautch girl
mukhiya	- village chief
naka	- crossing
nallahs	- channel for water
namaste	- Hindu greeting
nana	- maternal grandfather
octroi	- tax imposed on transiting goods by local municipality
Pangara	- Indian Coral (tree)
paratha	- shallow fried Indian bread
parikrama	- ritual of going around a holy place
pooja	- prayer ritual
poori bhaji	- popular food of potatoes and deep fried bread
prasad	- offering to God, distributed amongst devotees
punya	- good deed

rotis	- bread
razai	- thick blanket
rudraksha	- a Himalayan seed considered holy
sadhus	- holy men
salwaar	- trouser like loose garment
shabad	- couplets recited in Sikh gurudwaras
shikara	- boat
shlokas	- Sanskrit verses of spiritual value
som ras	- ancient name for alcohol
Sumo	- brand of SUV
thali	- typical Indian meal served on a steel plate
yagna	- ritual prayer to Fire God for favours
yatra	- journey
zamindar	- landlord
zindagee	- life

Acknowledgements

Many are those who helped me during the journey and in the three years it took to write *One Life to Ride.*

I thank Maj. Gen. (Retd.) M.S. Pillai, Surg. Cmde G. Vishwanath, Drs. Bharati and Rajesh Mehta, Kalyan, and Anita Paul for their assistance while I was on the road.

I sincerely acknowledge my wife Meena's support both during the trip and later while editing my writing. I thank Prof. Raj Rao, Head of Pune University's Department of English, for his creative writing course which taught me to 'Show-not-Tell'. Guitar Chatterjee for providing the key to a thought-lock. Brig. (Retd.) Vivek Sapatekar, VSM, and Nick Yapp for their useful tips which helped polish up the manuscript. I also thank my friends Dr. K. Krishnanand, Amodini Gagnavir, Dr. Promilla Butani, and my sister Nimmi for encouraging me to write.

Ajit Harisinghani returned to India from the US with a master's degree in speech pathology and long hair. Although he has long shed his hair, he still retains his profession and earns his living helping young adults and children overcome speech problems like stammering.

His other interests include sitting and staring at stars, cross-country motorcycling, writing and singing.

He lives in Pune and can be reached at singingyogi@yahoo.com.

Upcoming Writing:

I am currently working on a second travel book which is based on my solo motorcycle journey from Pune to Thimpu (Bhutan) in 2007.

On this journey, the author is in search of 'Happiness'– and thinks that Bhutan, with its unique concept of Gross National Happiness, might hold the key to this elusive secret.

The physically focused, solo motorcycle ride, which traverses India, beginning at sea-level and goes 3000 kms. north-east, through Maharashtra, Chattisgarh, Orissa, Jharkhand, Bihar to reach the world's newest democracy - Bhutan.

The other journey is the mind travelling through realms of memories, inferences and possibilities. There is always an element of mischief intertwined within events.

It is an attempt to read the universe and our place in its cosmic design. Our desires and the stress that we put ourselves through chasing their fulfilment. The guilt we reap from pleasure and the fear that we have of losing it all to that dreaded enemy - death.

The message here is that really, we are all okay. With all our little biological secrets and suppressed memories of things we can't now talk about, we are all fine just as we are today, right at this very moment of existence. The content attempts to entertain, empower, shock and perhaps even liberate!

Ajit Harisinghani
Pune, India